SOME NOTES ABOUT PST TOMOWO…

'Pastor Tomowo, my very close friend and sister, is my most spiritual female friend grounded in the ways and acts of God. I know undoubtedly that she does not only have God but knows and walks with Him intimately –and unto this, she's sold out. She lives a life of wholeness both on and off the pulpit'.

- Dr Oyinbo Manuel,
Resident Pastor, Kingsway International Christian Centre,
Windhoek, Namibia.

'Adetomowo Faduyile George is a Consultant Public Health Pharmacist turned Preacher. She is engraced with an unusual revelation of the scriptures. The messages of Tomowo are topical and heart-searching. She is blessed with deep Holy Ghost insight. She is a teacher of the Word and she ministers at conferences and seminars. Adetomowo is a gift from God to this generation!'

-Pastor Abraham Olufemi Ojeme,
Senior Pastor, Winners Chapel, Abuja, Nigeria

'Pastor tomowo is a trained consultant pharmacist who is fervent for the Lord. Her burning desire to reach people across geographical borders of nations through the Church in the Air has blessed many homes and individuals. May our Lord prosper her vision and continually renew her anointing'.

- Dr Kayode Afolabi,
Consultant Obstetrician and Gynaecologist,
Director, Reproductive Health, Federal Ministry of Health, Abuja, Nigeria

'I have known pastor tomowo for almost two years now. She loves God very dearly and she has a very good understanding of God's word that she teaches weekly. Focusing on contemporary topics and issues that are relevant to the needs of believers hungry for the truth of God's word and how to apply that truth in living out the Christian life victoriously in the 21st century''.

- Gabriel Okougha
Resident Pastor, KICC, The Fountain of Grace,
Gray, Essex, London, United Kingdom

'Pastor Tomowo is... A true lover of the Lord Jesus. Passionate about the kingdom of God. Committed to enlightening saints with the truth of Christ'.

- Pastor Bankie Olusina.
Kingdom –Word Ministries,
Enugu, Nigeria.

'I am being blessed by the messages by Pst Tomowo. They are very relevant, inspiring, and encouraging. Thank you, Pst Tomowo for your care for the body to share this with us. God bless you'.

- Randi Corkey.
Almond, New York, USA

PRAYER

DYNAMICS...

. . . a peep into the 'how' of praying

PRAYER DYNAMICS

...a peep into the 'how' of praying

pst tomowo

Prayer Dynamics...

[Maiden Edition]

©2020 pst tomowo

ISBN: 9781657040168

The church in the Air publications.

1192 Rising Moon Trail,

Snellville, GA, 30078, USA

Website: www.air.church

Email: info@air.church

Library of Congress Control Number:

2019920264

Publisher's note:

The reader should not regard the recommendations, ideas and lifestyle practices expressed and described in this book as a substitute for the advice of certified medical specialists or other professionals and experts. The application of such expressed therein is at the reader's sole discretion and risk.

UNTO GOD . . .

'Until now you have asked nothing in My name.

Ask, and you will receive, that your joy may be full'.

- John 16:24

CONTENTS···

OVERVIEW...

PRAYER DYNAMICS . . .

I sure have been a victim of praying and praying and praying... for many years with no results nor answers to show for my prayers! However, these many years of long-standing prayers gave me; the opportunity to try out many ways and how's of praying.

Until the Lord stepped in, in His Mercies, Thank GOD, He intervened, and showed me that it is 'Not by might nor by power, but by My Spirit'... Says the Lord of host.' (Zechariah 4:6 NKJV)

I sure have prayed...

Thank GOD, I waited; for what I now know, and the worth of what is currently shown me, worth all the waiting!

Prayer Dynamics... A peep into the 'HOW' of praying!

Many stumbled on answers to prayers and rejoiced; however, due to a lack of understanding of 'HOW' they got there, it becomes difficult to replicate the same in future needs.

There is the 'HOW' of praying... There are expected ways... *'Now this is the confidence that we have in Him, if we ask anything according to His will, He HEARS us, and if we know that He hears us, whatever we ask, we know that we have the petitions that we have asked of Him.' (1 John 5:14-15).*

What then is this 'Will of GOD in praying?

What is the 'HOW' in praying?

Is it possible to enjoy answers to prayers always?

All these, in Prayer Dynamics... a peep into the 'HOW' of praying.

Our GOD is GOOD, and HIS MERCIES endure forevermore, Amen. I pray that this Book BLESSES you as it is BLESSING us. Thank you.

pst tomowo

... setting men up with GOD, for a GLORIOUS TURNAROUND!

DIFFERENT TYPES & LEVELS OF PRAYERS

Prayer Dynamics ...

1. DIFFERENT TYPES AND LEVELS OF PRAYERS...

THE DIFFERENT TYPES AND LEVELS OF PRAYERS...

One day, our Lord JESUS CHRIST, when asked to teach how to pray, gave the disciples this model of Prayer...

THE LORD'S PRAYER...

' In this manner, therefore, pray: Our Father in heaven, hallowed be your name. Your Kingdom come. Your will be done on earth as it is in heaven. Give us this day our daily bread. And forgive us our debts, as we forgive our debtors. And do not lead us into temptation, but deliver us from the evil one. For yours is the Kingdom and the power and the glory forever. Amen. ' (Matthew 6:9-153 NKJV)

On another day, our Lord JESUS CHRIST gave a parable to this end that men ought always to pray... in other words, men should pray until their change come. Let us look at it below:

[1] "Then he spoke a parable to them, that men always ought to pray and not lose heart, [2] saying: "there was in a certain city a judge who did not fear GOD nor regard man. [3] Now there was a widow in that city; and she came to him, saying, 'get justice for me from my adversary.' [4] And he would not for a while; but afterward he said within himself, 'though I do not fear GOD nor regard man, [5] yet because this widow troubles me I will avenge her, lest by her continual coming she weary me."

[6]Then the Lord said, "Hear what the unjust judge said. [7] And shall GOD not avenge his own elect who cry out day and night to Him, though He bears long with them? [8] I tell you that he will avenge them speedily. Nevertheless, when the son of man comes, will He really find faith on the earth?" (Luke 18:1-8 NKJV).

Our Lord JESUS CHRIST says Faith is persisting in the place of prayers until your change comes.

Yet on another occasion, He charged the disciples to pray with high expectation to receive... He said, 'Have Faith in GOD'.

"So JESUS answered and said to them, "Have faith in GOD. For assuredly, I say to you, whoever says to this mountain, 'Be

17

removed and be cast into the sea,' and does not doubt in his heart, but believes that those things he says will be done, he will have whatever he says. Therefore I say to you, whatever things you ask when you pray, believe that you receive them, and you will have them.' (Mark 11:22-24 NKJV)

Yet on another occasion, when teaching the disciples on the mountain, He said:

'Ask, and it will be given you; seek, and you shall find; knock, and it will be opened to you. [8] For everyone who asks receives, and he who seeks finds, and to him who knocks it will be opened.' (Matthew 7:7-8 NKJV).

Here, He made it clear that some issues in life will require just asking... once you ask, it will be given to you. However, there are some issues that the ASK Key will not work for; you are to go for the SEEK Key, and if the Seek key refuses to crack it, then go for the KNOCK Key. In other words, please do not stop until it is done unto you.

Therefore, there are different kinds of prayers; used for different circumstances and situations... A pattern or type of Prayer will not work in all conditions and at all times. Understanding these diversities in prayers will always propel us to ask, what kind of Prayer am I to apply for this situation? For it is in getting it right with the type of Prayer that you are guaranteed a sure answer from GOD... Let us look at some different common kinds of prayers available to us today...

There are different kinds of prayers... And different levels of prayers... Let us take the Different types of Prayers first.

THE DIFFERENT KINDS OF PRAYERS...
I. PRAYER OF SALVATION...

The Prayer of Salvation is the expected very first Prayer of a believer. The prayer grants access to the Kingdom of God through CHRIST JESUS. At Salvation, an unbeliever confesses his sins, is convicted of them, asks GOD for forgiveness through the Blood of JESUS CHRIST, and calls upon the Name of JESUS CHRIST as their Lord and Saviour.

At Salvation, there is the PEACE of Deliverance, Righteousness in CHRIST, and deliverance from the dominion of darkness. This Prayer is said privately, alone, or in a gathering when a call for salvation is made at the altar or another Christian can lead it.

Many people can experience supernatural occurrences during this Prayer. It could be as simple as 'a feeling of warmth and peace'... Or as much as crying, physical manifestations like shouting, screaming with accompanying divine healing, deliverances, etc.

At Salvation comes PEACE, assurance of Salvation, a Longing and hunger for GOD, His word, and a new love for GOD and the things of the Kingdom of CHRIST. There is also a sudden disappearance of the affinity for sins, losing taste and desire to sin.

'For "whoever calls on the name of the Lord shall be saved. " *(Romans 10:13 KJV).*

'Therefore, if anyone is in Christ, he is a new creation; old things have passed away; behold, all things have become new.' (2 Corinthians 5:17 NKJV).

II. PRAYER OF SANCTIFICATION...

The Prayer of Sanctification is said by believers desiring a deeper walk with GOD. It is longing and requesting Divine visitation, dedication and consecration unto GOD in worship, service and spiritual upliftment. Any Christian can say this kind of Prayer at any time. It is setting oneself apart for the good and use of GOD.

'Or do you despise the riches of His goodness, forbearance, and longsuffering, not knowing that the goodness of God leads you to repentance?' (Romans 2:4 NKJV)

'My little children, of whom I travail in birth again until Christ be formed in you.' (Galatians 4:19 NKJV).

In the Prayer of sanctification, Christians travail in prayers until the fullness of Christ is formed in them. Search for the promises in the scriptures and be desirous of them, pray them, and meditate on them until they become your realities. The Bible says that God has BLESSED us with every spiritual blessing in heavenly places in Christ (Ephesians 1:3); however, this manifestation can only be born through prayers, called the Prayer of sanctification.

III. PRAYER OF DEDICATION...

The Prayer of Dedication is also called the Prayer of Consecration. It is the kind of Prayer when someone or something is consecrated to GOD. Such is when a man or woman is called apart for the work of the ministry. It is also said when an object, building, vehicle, or materials are dedicated unto God for His Gospel's sake.

'As they ministered to the Lord and fasted, the Holy Spirit said, "Now separate to Me Barnabas and Saul for the work to which I have called them." (Acts 13:2 NKJV)

IV. PRAYER OF PETITION...

The Prayer of Petition is the kind of Prayer where petitions or requests are made unto GOD. It is a prayer requesting GOD for something, such as 'GOD, give us Peace'... 'Give us our daily bread'... 'Heal our nation'... Prayer of petition is ongoing for regular and routine basic requests. It is the kind of Prayer our Lord JESUS CHRIST gave a model in Matthew 6:9-13; 'Our Father who art in heaven... Give us this day, our daily bread... Deliver us from evil...'

This kind of Prayer is desirous by GOD of His children. The Bible says you did not receive because you did not ask. Our Lord JESUS CHRIST says:

'Until now you have asked nothing in My name. Ask, and you will receive, that your joy may be full.' (John 16:24 NKJV).

V. PRAYER OF AGREEMENT...

The Prayer of Agreement is a kind of Prayer involving two or more believers. It is a prayer that requires two or more people to agree on an issue and pray unto GOD about this. Our LORD JESUS CHRIST says Heaven honours this kind of Prayer.

'Again I say to you that if two of you agree on earth concerning anything that they ask, it will be done for them by My Father in heaven. [20] For where two or three are gathered together in My name, I am there in the midst of them.' (Matthew 18:19-20 NKJV).

In agreement prayers, the parties involved must agree on the issues. The agreement is the highlight of this kind of Prayer. Agreeing requires unquestioning belief in GOD on a matter, deciding that GOD is able, and assenting to the power of the agreement prayer. Christian married couples can leverage this kind of Prayer. The marriage covenant gives room for many such prayer opportunities to the Glory of GOD.

VI. CORPORATE PRAYER...

Corporate Prayer is also a kind of agreement prayer; however, requiring a crowd of people. It is the kind of Prayer said in the churches. It could be a clarion call for a divine visitation for a change in a community, nation or among a people. In the early church, when the government killed one of the apostles and arrested the second one, Peter, the whole church raised their voice in prayers. GOD intervened, and Peter was released from prison miraculously afterwards.

[5]*'Peter was therefore kept in prison, but constant Prayer was offered to God for him by the church.* [6]*And when Herod was about to bring him out, that night Peter was sleeping, bound with two chains between two soldiers; and the guards before the door were keeping the prison.* [7] *Now behold, an angel of the Lord stood by him, and a light shone in the prison, and he struck Peter on the side and raised him up, saying, "Arise quickly!" And his chains fell off his hands'. (Acts 12:5-7 NKJV).*

This kind of Prayer has saved many situations in the church's history; it is still available and as powerful today.

VII. PRAYER OF WARFARE...

The Prayer of Warfare is a kind of Prayer where believers set out to war spiritually against the enemy of their souls. It requires some 'spiritual muscles', readily available for believers. The Bible says we are in a spiritual battle, constantly wrestling against the enemy of our souls.

'For we do not wrestle against flesh and blood, but against principalities, against powers, against the rulers of the darkness of this age, against spiritual hosts of wickedness in the heavenly places.' (Ephesians 6:12 NKJV).

'He has delivered us from the power of darkness and conveyed us into the kingdom of the Son of His love, in whom we have redemption through His blood, the forgiveness of sins.' (Colossians 1:13-14)

'For though we walk in the flesh, we do not war according to the flesh. ⁴ For the weapons of our warfare are not carnal but mighty in God for pulling down strongholds, casting down arguments and every high thing that exalts itself against the knowledge of God, ⁵ bringing every thought into captivity to the obedience of Christ. (2 Corinthians 10:3-5 NKJV).

In spiritual warfare, the prayers are said with authority, not begging or appealing to GOD to help... It is taking one's stand from the point of who we are in CHRIST, insisting on the finished works of CHRIST over the devil.

Rebuking the devil until he bows. Engaging the power of attorney to use the Name of our Lord JESUS CHRIST and the Blood of JESUS.

In spiritual warfare prayers, everything can be used as a weapon, the sea, the air, the land, water, clothing materials, etc. Haggai 2:6-9 says that GOD will shake the heavens, the sea, the dry land and the nations against the forces of darkness.

> *In spiritual warfare, the prayers are said with authority, not begging or appealing to GOD to help...*
>
> *It is taking one's stand from the point of who we are in CHRIST, insisting on the finished works of CHRIST over the devil.*

In this kind of Prayer, understanding who you are in CHRIST and the Believers' authority is key to successful spiritual warfare.

The Prayer is used when faced with demonic attacks, unexplainable evil, impending danger, witches and wizards' spells, etc. In this kind of Prayer, increasing one's knowledge of CHRIST boosts confidence to battle over the enemy.

VIII. PRAYER OF INTERCESSION...

The Prayer of Intercession is a kind of Prayer made for and on behalf of another person. As no one has absolute authority over another man's will, a prayer of intercession must be made for you to desire any change over another person's life.

In intercession, one stands in the gap for another. This Prayer can also be used when praying for nations, leaders, and the salvation of lost souls. The Prayer of intercession requires a resilience approach. It may be said for a very long time. It is not a prayer said once. It is a continuous prayer, which requires constant agonizing in the place of prayers for lost souls, family members, leaders and nations.

It is the kind of Prayer Our Lord JESUS CHRIST will often go all night long while on this earth...

'If my people who are called by My name will humble themselves, and pray and seek My face, and turn from their wicked ways, then I will hear from heaven, and will forgive their sin and heal their land.' (2 Chronicles 7:14 NKJV).

'And it came to pass in those days, that He (Jesus Christ) went out into a mountain to pray, and continued all night in prayer to God.' (Luke 6:12 KJV).

This kind of Prayer can be made individually as intercessors, as a group, community, or nation, in a prayer meeting, or as a clarion call for a change in their land.

'Blow a trumpet in Zion, consecrate a fast, Call a sacred assembly.' (Joel 2:15 NKJV).

This type of Prayer can and should be said by all Christians for the leaders, nations and salvation of their loved ones. However, there are people in the church that are explicitly called to stand in the gap for leaders, churches, communities and nations. They are the Intercessors; they tarry day and night until there is a change in the land.

Before our Lord JESUS CHRIST was born, some prophets were sealed and bound alive until they saw the arrival of our Lord and Saviour. Simeon and Anna declared during the dedication of child JESUS their devotion to seeing His Salvation:

[29]*'Lord, Now You are letting Your servant depart in Peace, According to your word,* [30] *For my eyes have seen Your Salvation,* [31] *Which You have prepared before the face of all peoples...'* (Luke 2:29-31 NKJV).

They were intercessors for the fulfilment of GOD's promise and salvation of Israel at the time.

IX. PRAYER OF FAITH...

The Prayer of Faith is the kind of Prayer that requires standing in agreement with the word of GOD and birthing such a promise into physical reality. This kind of Prayer is the bedrock of all prayers. All other types of Prayer will be effective when faith is intact. It is a must kind of Prayer for all Christians. For without Faith, it is impossible to please GOD. None of the above prayers can be successful without the Prayer of Faith.

However, this also is the least understood kind of Prayer. Many people today ask this question... 'Why is GOD not answering my prayers? The question to ask in answering that would be... 'How is your Prayer of Faith skill?' For this is the 'HOW' of praying. Breakthrough and a good understanding of the Prayer of Faith will make a believer a success in life and destiny.

Many people stumble on the Prayer of faith and get results and answers to their prayers. However, because they lack the understanding of how they got it right, it becomes difficult to replicate it in other prayer needs.

Faith is the bedrock of all prayers... Your understanding of the Prayer of faith and its application will make you successful in any other type of Prayer.

Many people stumble on the Prayer of faith and get results and answers to their prayers. However, because they lack the understanding of how they got it right, it becomes difficult to replicate it in other prayer needs.

The Prayer of Faith is the 'HOW' of prayers... for the scriptures repeat the importance of this: 'The just shall live by faith', and 'Without faith, you cannot please GOD'... The prophet of old revealed the intention of GOD to make the Prayer of faith the bedrock of Christianity, saying:

'Behold the proud, His soul is not upright in him; But the just shall live by his faith.' (Habakkuk 2:4 NKJV).

> **This Prayer of faith is the 'HOW' of prayers...**

When the appointed time came, and our Lord JESUS CHRIST came into the scene, He reiterated this by saying in Mark 11:22, *'Have Faith in GOD.'*... And to further emphasize this to the heirs of salvation, we, the Christians, the Spirit of the Lord, repeat this truth in the inspired letters written to the church in Romans 1:17; Galatians 3:11 and Hebrews 10:38.

'Now the just shall live by faith; But if anyone draws back, My soul has no pleasure in him.' (Hebrews 10:38 NKJV).

It is, therefore, a worthy venture to settle down and understand what Faith is and is not. How does one apply the Prayer of faith to different life circumstances, and how to please GOD in Faith?

... It is against this backdrop that **Prayer Dynamics** is born!

X. PRAYER OF HOPE...

The Prayer of Hope is the kind of prayer we make in assurance and anticipation of our inheritance in CHRIST JESUS at the end of the age. It is a prayer all believers should pray regularly, being fully confident that He that began the good work in us will perform it until the end—having the hope that when CHRIST shall appear, we shall be like Him and ascend with Him. The confidence that the Holy Spirit in us is our guarantee of redemption, our seal of redemption.

'Being confident of this very thing, that He who begun a good work in you will complete it until the day of Jesus Christ.' (Philippians 1:6 NKJV).

'For whatever things were written before were written for our learning, that we through the patience and comfort of the Scriptures might have hope.' (Romans 15:4 NKJV)

'In hope of eternal life, which God, who cannot lie, promised before time began.' (Titus 1:2 NKJV).

'Let us hold fast the confession of our hope without wavering, for He who promised is faithful.' (Hebrews 10:23 NKJV).

'In Him you also trusted, after you heard the word of truth, the gospel of your salvation, in whom also, having believed, you were sealed with the Holy Spirit of promise, who is the guarantee of our inheritance until the redemption of the purchased possession, to the praise of His glory.' (Ephesians 1:13-14)

The above and some more are prayers we pray in the hope of our eternal life in CHRIST JESUS...

Your Notes . . .

The different types of Prayers... Which of them are you engaging often? And why?

DIFFERENT LEVELS OF PRAYERS...

There are also different levels of Prayers. Our Lord JESUS CHRIST revealed this in Matthew 7:7-8 when He said that we should Ask, Seek, or Knock.

[7] *'Ask, and it will be given you; seek, and you shall find; knock, and it will be opened to you.* [8] *For everyone who asks receives, and he who seeks finds, and to him who knocks it will be opened.'* *(Matthew 7:7-8 NKJV).*

Our Lord JESUS CHRIST reveals through this scripture the different levels of prayers we can embark on in practice. The Asking level, the Seeking level, and the Knocking level.

I. THE ASK LEVEL...

He emphasized that some situations require your Asking... as simple as this is, answers are granted to you. However, there are some situations that the Ask Key will not work for; He urges us to take it to the next level, SEEK...

II. THE SEEK LEVEL...

At the Seeking level, beyond asking, the believer may need to seek more understanding, information and attention from GOD to combat the challenging situations. Many may fast, seek Divine counsel, and seek agreement with higher Anointing, such as with the man or woman of GOD over him or her. At this level of Prayer, many miracles are born. However, this Seek Key will not answer some situations. Our Lord JESUS CHRIST says we move to the next level, KNOCK.

III. THE KNOCK LEVEL...

At the Knock level, situations and circumstances that seem to defile all prayers and waiting are addressed. People say, 'I have prayed and prayed and prayed and prayed'... 'I have been to many men of God to lay a hand on me to no avail'. This level is where Our Lord JESUS CHRIST says, KNOCK ... despite the opposing prevailing circumstances, KNOCK... He says the ability to insist at this KNOCK level until your change comes is called Faith in Luke 18:6...

[7] 'And shall God not avenge His own elect who cry out day and night to Him, though He bears long with them? [8] I tell you that He will avenge them speedily. Nevertheless, when the Son of Man comes, will He really find faith on the earth?' (Luke 18:7-8 NKJV).

Our Lord JESUS CHRIST ascribes this level of Prayer, KNOCK, as the level of Faith. The question I asked for a very long time was... 'Why does GOD bear long with His elect before He answers them speedily? Why that waiting? Hmmmmmm...

This is Prayer Dynamics...

This Book, therefore, will focus on this kind of Prayer... THE PRAYER OF FAITH as it is the bedrock for all other categories and types of prayers. In the MERCIES of GOD, we will be looking into the WHY of waiting in praying. How are we sure we are in Prayer of Faith and not Hope? What will trigger Heaven's response to answer us speedily... and so on?

We pray that the Mercies of GOD prevail for you, granting you insight and revelation in the Knowledge of CHRIST in the Name of YESHUA HAMASHIACH (JESUS CHRIST), Amen.

Your Notes . . .

The different levels of prayers: The Ask, The Seek and The Knock Levels... What level will you classify your present prayer points?

Prayer Dynamics ...

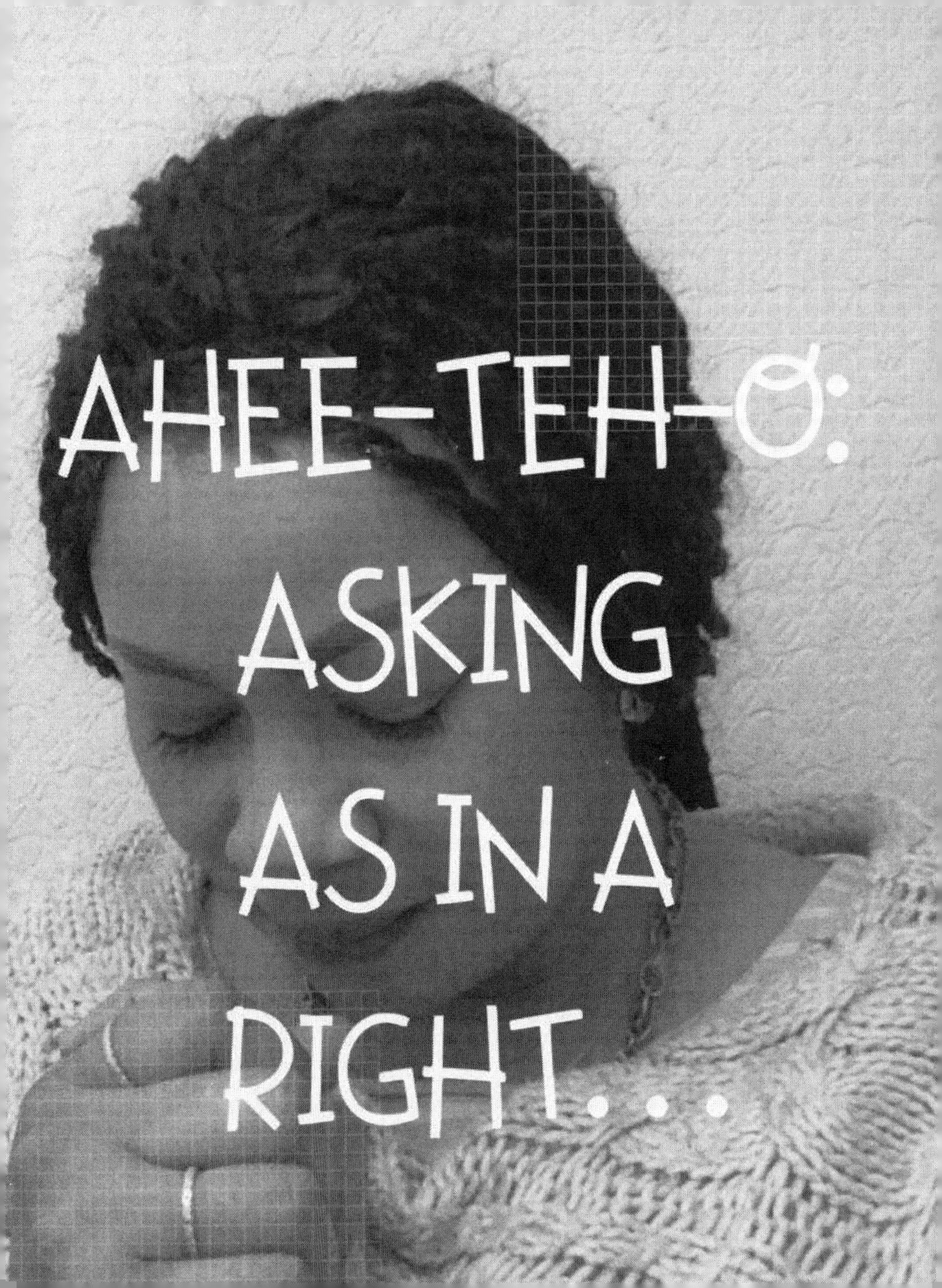
AHEE-TEH-Ó:
ASKING
AS IN A
RIGHT....

Prayer Dynamics ...

2. AHEE-TEH-O: ASKING AS IN A RIGHT···

AHEE-TEH-O... ASKING AS IN A RIGHT!

WHAT IS AHEE-TEH-O?

*O*ne day, the Spirit of GOD revealed something to me from these scriptures below: the word ASK!

"Therefore I say to you, whatever things you <u>ask</u> when you pray, believe that you receive them, and you will have them." (Mark 11:24 NKJV)

'<u>Ask</u> and it will be given to you; seek, and you will find; knock, and it will be opened to you... For everyone who <u>asks</u> receives, and he who seeks finds, and to him who knocks, it will be opened (Matthew 7:7-8).

40

The word ASK here in Greek is pronounced as AHEE-TEH-O. It is a special kind of ask... It does not mean the regular ASK... therefore, I searched it out. What is unique about the word ASK in the scriptures above? Let us see what we got:

Just like some English words may mean different things, such as the word STAR could mean an astronomical object; it could also be used to refer to a celebrated achiever ... ASK was used in the new testament to mean different things...

There are five kinds of ASK used in the New Testament; they are Ask: as a matter of information; Ask: as a request for a favour; Ask: as strictly a demand for something due to you; Ask: as a search for something hidden... and Ask: as an idea of urgent need, hence a petition...

Surprisingly, all scriptures that talk of asking in Faith for something reflect the third one. Ask: strictly as a demand for something due to you...

This is how our Lord JESUS CHRIST wants us to Ask... not begging, instead, asking as it were, a demand for something due to you.

Before we look at this special Ask called AHEE-TEH-O... Let us see how the other ASKs are used in the Gospel. When used in prayers, these others do not yield the expected results.

I. ASK -AS A MATTER OF INFORMATION, MAINLY

A certain blind man sitting by the road begging, when he heard the multitude passing by, he ASKED, what means this...

35 'Then it happened, as He was coming near Jericho, that a certain blind man sat by the road begging. 36 And hearing a multitude passing by, he asked what it meant.' (Luke 18:35-36 NKJV)

A nobleman whose son our Lord JESUS CHRIST healed, as he was on his way home, his servant told him his son lives... then He asked (inquired), what hour he began to amend...

'So he asked them at what time he began to get better. They said, 'Yesterday during the seventh hour (1 p.m.), the fever left him.' (John 4:52 AMP). The man's son's health was restored when our Lord JESUS CHRIST prayed for him.

One day, as our Lord JESUS CHRIST was informing His disciples of the kind of death he will face and of his betrayal by one of them, Simon Peter beckons on John to ask ... Who is to betray Him...

23 'Now there was leaning on Jesus' bosom one of His disciples, whom Jesus loved. 24 Simon Peter therefore motioned to him to ask who it was of whom He spoke.' (John 13:23-24 NKJV).

These scriptures above use ASK for mere inquiring, mainly for information's sake. Not recommended for use in prayers.

II. ASK -AS A REQUEST FOR A FAVOUR...

This type of ASK is used for requesting a favour from someone. Surprisingly, Christians often use this type of ASK when asking GOD for something, which is why they do not receive their answers because anytime you use this ASK, the Lord does not hear you.

Let us see how it is being used in the Gospel...

JESUS asked his disciples... Who do men say I, the son of man is? .... *'When Jesus came into the region of Caesarea Philippi, He asked His disciples, saying, 'Who do men say that I, the Son of Man, am?' (Matthew 16:13 NKJV).*

One day, our Lord JESUS entered Simon's boat and prayed him to thrust out a bit so He could preach from Peter's boat... *'Then He got into one of the boats, which was Simon's, and asked him to put out a little from the land. And He sat down and taught the multitudes from the boat.' (Luke 5:3 NKJV).*

This one is very interesting... A Syro-Phoenician woman (A Greek, not a Jew) kept asking our Lord JESUS to deliver her demon-possessed daughter... Our Lord JESUS did not answer her at first, and then his disciples implored him to...

(Our Lord, JESUS did not answer her because she was not using AHEE-TEH-O... She was asking, seeking for favour... This type was a wrong ASK for a miracle. To help her change to the right ASK... AHEE-TEH-O, '*He told her that 'Let the children be filled first, for it is not good to take the children's bread and throw it to the little dogs.''* (Mark 7:27 NKJV)

She, however, in the mercies of GOD, got the revelation, and shifted from asking for favour... to demanding for a right... she said: '*And she answered and said to Him, 'Yes, Lord, yet even the little dogs under the table eat from the children's crumbs.'* (Mark 7:28 NKJV).

> **Today, many believers are stuck with their long-aged prayers because they are using the wrong ASK...**

This statement shifted her request from seeking a favour to demanding a right! And this time, she got what she wanted... Our Lord JESUS CHRIST told her... '*Then He said to her, 'For this saying, go your way, the demon has gone out of your daughter.'* (Mark 7:29 NKJV). SELAH: Pause, ponder and think about this...

Today, many believers are stuck with their long-aged prayers because they are using the wrong ASK... Until she found herself with a right... '*Even the little dogs under the table eat from the children's crumbs*'... Only then that she receive her answers... Hmmmmmm.... Food for thought!

III. ASK -STRICTLY AS A DEMAND FOR SOMETHING DUE TO YOU: (AHEE-TEH-O)

The 'AHEE-TEH-O' is the only type of ASK that we are to use when praying in Faith. It is the only kind of ASK that GOD hears and answers concerning requesting for something from the Lord. It is the type of ASK in Faith. This ASK is used in the following scriptures...

'_Ask, and it will be given to you; seek, and you will find; knock, and it will be opened to you. ⁸For everyone who asks receives, and he who seeks finds, and to him who knocks it will be opened.'_ (Matthew 7:7-8 NKJV)

> **Anytime you ask GOD for something, you are to pad it with a right for the request. If you do not see yourself as deserving it ... GOD may not answer you.**

'_Again I say to you that if two of you agree on earth concerning anything that they ask, it will be done for them by My Father in heaven.'_ (Matthew 18:19 NKJV)

'_Therefore I say to you, whatever things you ask when you pray, believe that you receive them, and you will have them.'_ (Mark 11:24 NKJV)

'_If you ask anything in My name, I will do it.'_ (John 14:14 NKJV)

'Until now you have <u>asked</u> nothing in My name, <u>Ask</u>, and you will receive, that your joy may be full.' (John 16:24 NKJV).

'And when Herodias' daughter herself came in and danced, and pleased Herod and those who sat with him, the king said to the girl, '<u>Ask</u> me whatever you want, and I will give it to you.' 21 He also swore to her, 'Whatever you <u>ask</u> me, I will give you, up to half of my kingdom.'' (Mark 9:22-23 NKJV).

> **AHEE-TEH-O. Asking strictly as demanding for a right due you…. Think about this!**

King Herod also understood this kind of Ask... and used it for his daughter, which led to the death of John the Baptist...

AHEE-TEH-O. Asking strictly as demanding for a right due you... Think about this...

These scriptures above on prayers focus on asking GOD in Faith. However, it is an ASK with a difference... It must include a right, strictly demanding for something due to you. It is the ASK our Lord JESUS CHRIST wants us to use anytime we request something from GOD. Think about this... Anytime you ask GOD for something, you must 'pad' it with a right for the request. If you do not see yourself as deserving it... GOD may not answer you. AHEE-THE-O... Asking strictly as a demand for something due you...

Prayer Dynamics... AHEE-TEH-O: Asking strictly as a demand for something due you. My dear friend, what will you rather do with this information? Let us see the remaining types of Ask used in the Gospel.

IV. ASK -AS A SEARCH FOR SOMETHING HIDDEN:

This kind of Ask implies searching for something hidden. It is not for prayers in Faith; it is asking as a search for something out of sight. Examples are:

'Ask and it will be given you, <u>seek</u>, and you will find, knock, and it will be opened to you. (Matthew 7:7b NKJV). The word SEEK is translated as asking in search of something hidden.

'While He was still talking to the multitudes, behold, His mother and brothers stood outside, <u>seeking</u> to speak with him.' (Matthew 12: 46 NKJV). Here, SEEKING is translated as Asking in search of something hidden. Also, *' And when they had found Him, they said unto Him, All men <u>seek</u> for thee.' (Mark 1: 37 KJV).*

V. ASK -AS AN IDEA OF URGENT NEED, A PETITION...

Our Lord JESUS CHRIST, employing the disciples to pray for more labourers for the work of the Gospel, as a regular, ongoing prayer said: *'Then He said to His disciples, 'The harvest truly is plentiful, but the laborers are few. [38]Therefore <u>pray</u> the Lord of harvest to* *send out laborers into His harvest.'' (Matthew 9:37-38 NKJV).* The word PRAY in this scripture is translated Ask as a petition for an urgent need.

A man whose son was possessed by demons went to the disciples of our Lord JESUS CHRIST, and they could not help him. When he saw the master, he narrated his ordeal: *'So I implored your disciples to cast it out, but they could not.' (Luke 9:40 NKJV).* The word IMPLORED here translated as Ask... as a petition for an urgent need.

Apostle Paul writing to the Romans used this type of Ask... *'making request if, by some means, now at last I may find a way in the will of God to come to you. (Romans 1:10 NKJV).* The word REQUEST is translated Ask... as a petition for an urgent need.

In the Prayer of faith, the only ASK we are expected to use is the AHEE-TEH-O: Asking: strictly as a demand for something due... Until you understand that what you are asking for is something due to you... you may not secure the attention of heaven. **Until you have a right that you deserve what you are asking for, these scriptures... Mark 11:24, Matt 7:7, Matt 18:18, John 14:14, John 16:24... will not work for you...**

How can one be confident that what is asked is a demand for something due? Let us see the amplified rendering of the verse *"for this reason I am telling you, whatever things you ask for in prayer [in accordance with GOD's will], believe [with confident trust] that you have received them, and they will be given to you." (Mark 11:24 AMP).*

When you ask in accordance with GOD's will... Then you are AHEE-TEH-O... When you ask in the confidence of your right to ask... Then you are AHEE-TEH-O... When you ask in the confidence of the authority you carry... Then you are AHEE-TEH-O...

HOW THEN SHOULD YOU ASK...?

Before you ask GOD for something, Ask yourself the following questions...

- What I'm asking for... Is it in line with GOD's will? (In line with His Word)

If you ask anything in My Name... (John 14:14). Is it asked in the Name of JESUS CHRIST? By his stripes... You were healed... (1 Peter 2:24); If His stripes healed me, then Healing is GOD's will for me. If we pray according to His will... He hears us... When He hears, then He answers... (1 John 5:14-15)

- Am I Qualified to Ask?

King Herod's daughter danced and was confident that her father would do whatever she asked... (Mk 6:23-25).

As believers, we partake in GOD's righteousness... Right standing with GOD qualifies us to ask. As many as receive JESUS... To them gave He, power to become the sons of GOD... John 1:12. This sonship qualifies any Christian.

And as Sons... GOD put the Spirit of his Son into us... Crying Abba, Father... (Galatians 4:6). Because of the Spirit of CHRIST in me, I qualify to ask.

- Do I have the Authority to Ask?

In salvation... We are given this authority:

In Mark 16:17-18... Our Lord JESUS CHRIST gave the believers the authority to use His Name. These signs shall follow those that believe... In My Name, they shall...

If you can answer the above questions on why you qualify for the request you are asking GOD for, then you can confidently AHEE-TEH-O by Asking as demand for what is due.

Once this step is settled, you are on your way to victorious and triumphant prayer life.

AHEE-TEH-O... Asking strictly as a demand for something due you. Until you find a reason and a right to what you desire, you have not started to pray. Think about this...

Your Notes:

AHEE-TEH-O: Asking as in a right for something due you... DO you see yourself as deserving what you are asking GOD for today? How?

PREPARATIONS FOR PRAYERS…

Prayer Dynamics ...

3. PRAYER DYNAMICS: PREPARATIONS FOR PRAYERS

WHY PREPARATIONS FOR PRAYERS...

We have by the GRACE of GOD looked into the different kinds or types of Prayers... Consecration, Agreement, Intercession, Faith...etc., and go by different ways of praying. We have also looked into the different levels of prayers, the ASK, SEEK and KNOCK levels of prayers (Matthew 7:7). By the Grace of GOD, we have also looked at the way to ASK, in prayers... It is now time to take these to the next level....

Some prayers require mere asking, and you get the answers; others need Seeking, extra praying, fasting, or laying on hands... However, there are some prayers for which the Ask and Seek keys will not work. These require a walk of Faith, enduring in Faith until a change is born. (Luke 18:6-8).

These kinds of prayers that require the KNOCK KEY give us the responsibility to understand how Faith works. It is this Prayer of Faith that the Just are to live by in life, through which we can only please GOD. This persistent Prayer that takes NO for an answer operates by skills that must be learnt and practised to apply effectively. My Father in the Lord, [1]Bishop David Oyedepo of Living Faith Church, Worldwide, taught extensively on this kind of Faith. In many of his messages, he defines Faith as:

'Faith is a spiritual partnership with the invisible GOD, thereby empowering us to do exploits.'

'Faith is putting GOD's Word to work and believing.'

'Faith is being fully persuaded of the Truth... the prevailing circumstances notwithstanding... until the Truth prevails....'

'Faith is our access to the Realms of Glory.'

I sincerely recommend the Word of Faith Bible Institute of Living Faith Church; it is a great Blessing.

Therefore, in Effective Praying, there is a need to prepare for prayers. Lack of preparation for prayers leads to shipwreck in prayer life. What is Preparation for Prayers, and why Preparation for Prayers?

---

[1] Bishop David Oyedepo, Living Faith Church. www.faithtabernacle.org.ng

WHAT ARE PREPARATIONS FOR PRAYERS...?

One day, the Spirit of God revealed to me that preparations are needed for successful prayer life. Praying and operational prayer life is serious business. Praying with the guarantee of answers is a 'serious' business that every believer should experience. However, inadequate preparations can lead to failure in Prayers.

WHAT ARE TO BE PREPARED FOR IN PRAYERS?

In preparations for Prayers, you must:

I. IDENTIFY THE KINDS OF PRAYERS YOU ARE INTO...

What kind of Prayer are you engaged in; Agreement prayers? Intercession for someone else? Corporate Prayers? Prayer of consecration, or Prayer of Faith.

Understanding the kind of Prayer is key to how the Prayer will be said.

II. IDENTIFY THE LEVEL OF PRAYERS YOU ARE IN...

Identifying the level you are at in your Prayer is also crucial. Have you started at all? Will it require just asking GOD for it? Is the situation requiring a Seek key, meaning will you need an increased level of attention, such as fasting, seeking knowledge and seeking higher Anointing? Or is the situation defiling all 'possible answers' yet? Will it require a Knock key?

When you settle down and diagnose the level of Prayer you are to engage in, it will help you set the desired Goal and push needed to achieve it. This stage is preparation for prayers. Getting it right at this stage is key to successful and effective prayer life.

III. IDENTIFY THE WORD OF GOD YOU ARE USING FOR PRAYERS...

At this stage, you also identify the word of GOD you are standing on for your prayers. Why determine a Word? 1 John 5:14-15 states clearly that GOD only hears if we ask according to His will. The word of GOD is the language of GOD. Without the Word of GOD, prayers will become amiss.

[14] 'Now this is the confidence that we have in Him, that if we ask anything according to His will, He hears us. [15] And if we know that He hears us, whatever we ask, we know that we have the petitions that we have asked of Him.' (1 John 5:14-15 NKJV).

Without the Word of GOD relating to the circumstances you want to pray about, your prayers are set to fail. Identifying the Word of God will give you the confidence to know that you are asking using the AHEE-TEH-O kind of asking... It gives you the confidence that you are asking strictly for something due you... It gives you a right to your claims… It assures you that you deserve what you are requesting.

The Good news, however, is… Your Name is written inside the Bible… Yes! Your circumstances are well spelt out inside the Bible. Nothing anyone is going through or desiring to become that does not have a reference in the Holy Scriptures… It is your responsibility to search it out!

'It is the Glory of God to conceal a matter, but the honour of kings is to search out a matter. (Proverbs 25:2 KJV)

> **Nothing anyone is going through or desiring to become that does not have a reference in the Holy Scriptures… It is now your responsibility to search it out.**

'You search the Scriptures, for in them you think you have eternal life, and these are they which testify of Me.' (John 5:39 NKJV).

'Search from the Book of the Lord, and read: Not one of these shall fail; Not one shall lack her mate. For my mouth has commanded it, and his Spirit has gathered them.' (Isaiah 34:16 NKJV).

It is your responsibility to sit down and search where your Name is and what the Bible says about your situation and your desired

expectation. Get a Bible app, click the Search, and type your case or your expected desire... For example, type in healing, breakthrough, open doors, deliverance... and tons of scriptures will come up... Settle down, and read them all until you find two or three that resonate well with you... That becomes your scriptures... That is your Name in the scriptures... Then and only then you are ready to pray...

When you have identified the scriptures you will be standing on in prayers, write them out. For you will need them soon. For the scriptures say by the mouth of two or three witnesses, every word shall be established.

'This will be the third time I am coming to you. 'By the mouth of two or three witnesses every word shall be established.' (2 Corinthians 13:1 NKJV)

'Therefore, endeavour to get at least two or three scriptures to use in your prayers, do not stand only on one. If you search very well, you will see at least two or three. It is also an excellent opportunity to ask the Holy Spirit to help you discover the scriptures to stand on.

This step is easy if you have been a habitual scripture reading and studying person as a Christian. However, if you are new to this, it is an excellent time to become a 'nerd' for the scriptures... use the Bible app, and get scriptures to work with in life.

Remember, GOD will only HEAR His Will, which is the Word of GOD. Until then, GOD will simply not hear you. The word of GOD is the language of GOD... when you speak the Word of GOD, you are speaking the language of GOD, and you can be sure that HE will hear you! With your scriptures at hand, you are ready for effective prayers!

IV. BROODING ON THE SCRIPTURES TO GAIN ACCESS TO THE WORD OF GOD...

The preparatory stage is also a time to brood on the scriptures you have identified for your prayers. This meditation is very important because the letters of scriptures alone are not powerful; the Word of GOD is hidden inside the scripture, and accessing the hidden Word is what guarantees the creation of your desired miracles.

> *'The Word of GOD is not just the Bible, the Word of GOD is hidden inside the Bible, and you need to dig deep to encounter it...*

One day the Spirit of GOD told me, 'The Word of GOD is not just the Bible; the Word of GOD is hidden inside the Bible, and you need to dig deep to encounter it.' Food for thoughts! The Bible says that the letter kills, and the Spirit gives life. You will not have Life until you assess the Spirit from the Bible.

60

'who also made us sufficient as ministers of the new covenant, not of the letter but of the Spirit, for the letter kills, but the Spirit gives life.' (2 Corinthians 3:6 NKJV)

The Scriptures further admonish that we spend time meditating on the Word ... Then, we can discover what is in it, thereby making our way prosperous.

'This Book of the Law shall not depart from your mouth, but you shall meditate in it day and night, that you may observe to do according to all that is written in it. For then you will make your way prosperous, and then you will have good success.' (Joshua 1:8)

Still, in preparation for prayers, you are to spend quality time on your identified scriptures and begin to meditate, brooding on them, until you lay hold on the Spirit of life therein.

> ***If you are not seeing the realities of the manifestation of the Word of GOD in your life, it is because probably you did not encounter the Spirit of the Word of Life. You were only quoting the Letter, also called logos of the word.***

Pst tomowo, all of these for prayers? Yes... not accessing the Word of life from the scriptures gives a false presentation that we believe the scriptures; however, we wonder why the scriptures are not working. THE WORD WORKS... May the Word begin to work for you from today in the Name of Yeshua Hamasiach (Jesus Christ), Amen.

If you are not seeing the realities of the manifestation of the Word of GOD in your life, it is because probably you did not encounter the Spirit of the Word of Life. You were only quoting the Letter, also called logos of the word.

Until you encounter the Life from the Word, also called Rhema, you will not experience the creative ability of the Word as stated in Hebrews 4:12.

'For the word of God is living and powerful, and sharper than any two-edged sword, piercing even to the division of soul and spirit, and of joints and marrow, and is a discerner of the thoughts and intents of the heart.

[13]And there is no creature hidden from His sight, but all things are naked and open to the eyes of Him to whom we must give account.' (Hebrews 4:12-13 NKJV).

Think about this ... There is no one and no situation the Word of GOD cannot fix. Absolutely nothing! However, it would be best to dig deep into the scriptures to encounter the actual Word... Rhema... The Spirit of the Word of Life...

V. CREATE AND MAINTAIN THE RIGHT ATMOSPHERE FOR GOD'S MANIFESTATION

Still, on Preparations for Prayers, this is an excellent time to begin to prepare and prop your atmosphere for miracles. GOD operates only in the right atmosphere. **Although GOD is omnipresent, His manifested presence is not everywhere.** He gave the earth to be ruled by man. Therefore, whenever GOD's presence is desired, man has to create it, or rather create an enabling environment for GOD's manifestation.

Everyone carries with them an atmosphere, an aura, a presence; some are of darkness, and others Light. As a default, the Bible says the darkness covers the earth, and gross darkness the people. Hence, by default, your atmosphere permits the works of darkness, not God. Therefore, to manifest Light, there must be a conscious effort to make that happen.

'For behold, the darkness shall cover the earth, And deep darkness the people; But the Lord will arise over you, And His glory will be seen upon you.' (Isaiah 60:2 NKJV).

Despite the dark atmosphere looming on the earth, the Lord will arise over you, and His Glory will be seen upon you. This atmosphere, however, is consciously activated by Faith. It will not happen to you automatically; it is your believing that birth it.

How then do we create the right atmosphere for GOD's Glory?

In our Book... 'JESUS CHRIST...my Substitute, my Sacrifice, my Inheritance'; we dealt extensively with how to create the right atmosphere for GOD's Glory. We have an exercise called 'The Almighty Formula'... This exercise helps in creating GOD's Presence in people's life... It consists of the following:

THE ALMIGHTY FORMULA... 30 MINS HIGH PRAISE ... + 30 MINS WAITING ON THE WORD OF GOD...+ 30 MINS MINGLING WITH THE HOLY SPIRIT ... EVERY DAY!

This practice is simply an exercise we use in our ministry to help

> **THE ALMIGHTY FORMULA...**
> **30 MINS HIGH PRAISE ...**
> **+**
> **30 MINS WAITING ON THE WORD OF GOD...**
> **+**
> **30 MINS MINGLING WITH THE HOLY SPIRIT ...**
> **EVERY DAY!**

engage the Presence of GOD. You may want to try it. You can also use your style of creating the right atmosphere for the Presence of GOD. Why do we need the right atmosphere in preparation for prayers? The Spirit of God will only operate in the Light zone. At the instant of sins and darkness, GOD will be gone. Hence to have a successful prayer, it is time to prop your atmosphere to carry GOD. Miracles, Divine visitations, and encounters only happen in the atmosphere of Light.

Therefore, create the right atmosphere for your desired miracles to occur before your face. Amen.

VI. ABSTINENCE FROM SINS

Finally, from our end, another vital thing to set in order when desiring a prayer is to abstain from sins.

The prayers of a sinner GOD will not hear. You cannot continue to sin and expect GOD to answer your prayers. In our Book... 'Understanding the works of darkness,' we dealt extensively on what are the multitude of sins, the affinity for sins and the way of escape from sins and their affinity. We learnt that Sin is a sure entrance to the darkness.

You cannot continue in Sin and expect your prayers to be heard. There is no exception to this rule. If you are into sins or cover your sins or un-repented of them, no matter who you are, GOD will not hear you.

In some cases, people under the covering of God's Inherited Goodness earned through the sacrificial life of worship of their past parents may seem like they are getting away with many sins and lawlessness... These people are benefiting from a Goodness they never created. With time, however, their children and children's children will reap the consequences of their rebelliousness and lawlessness. For though hands join in hands, a sinner shall not be unpunished, says the scriptures!

This is why, in preparation for prayers, staying clear of sins is a must for everyone, your proximity to the church notwithstanding!

'Now we know that God does not hear sinners, but if anyone is a worshiper of God and does His will, He hears him.' (John 9:31 NKJV)

'Though hand join in hand, the wicked shall not be unpunished: but the seed of the righteous shall be delivered.' (Proverbs 11:21 KJV)

> *To enter the throne of Grace for GRACE... Your Password is MERCY'*

GOD simply does not hear sinners' prayers!

Therefore, in preparation for prayers, sins must be dealt with; The Adamic sinful nature, the inherited sins from the past parents and the self-acquired sins. If we confess our sins and repent from them, we have the opportunity to be cleansed by the Blood of JESUS CHRIST and obtain Grace to help in time of need.

Hebrews 4:16 says, 'Come boldly to the throne of Grace to obtain Mercy, and find Grace to help in time of need.'

One day, the Spirit of God revealed to me that to enter the throne of Grace for GRACE... Your Password is MERCY'

'Anytime you sin, just go genuinely and say, LORD, I AM SORRY ... that is your password; you received a cleansing, so the enemy does not gain access into your life; in addition, just before you leave, you RECEIVE SOME PORTION OF GRACE... to help you in future needs!

(This is an extract from our Book: JESUS CHRIST, my Substitute, my Sacrifice, my Inheritance).

SELAH: Pause, ponder and think about this!

GOD does not operate in an atmosphere of sins; hence in preparation for prayers, go for cleansing by the Blood of Our Lord JESUS CHRIST...

These are just the beginning of praying effectively. Many people stop here in their prayer journey... and wonder why they did not get answers to their prayers... It is because they are still at the preparatory stage in Prayers. They have not started praying yet.

There may be more; however, if you can put the above-listed points in order, we believe you are now ready for prayers; a prayer that will birth answers; guaranteed... We will now move to the next step in Prayer Dynamics... The point of Faith...

Your Notes . . .

Why do we need to prepare for Prayers?

Your Notes . . .

How will you prepare for your pressing prayer point today?

THE POINT OF FAITH ...

Prayer Dynamics ...

4. PRAYER DYNAMICS: THE POINT OF FAITH···

BOILING POINT IN PRAYERS?... WHAT IS IT?

*T*his is the 'Boiling Point' in Prayers. A point of contacting Faith during Prayers... What is this Boiling Point? Let us see what the scriptures say about the Point of Faith...

WHAT IS THE POINT OF FAITH...?

[23] *"let us hold fast the confession of our hope without wavering, for he who promised is faithful.*

[35] *Therefore do not cast away your confidence, which has great reward.* [36] *For you have need of endurance, so that after you have done the will of God, you may receive the promise:* [37] *"for yet a little while, and he who is coming will come and will not tarry.* [38] *Now the just shall live by faith; but if anyone draws back, my soul has no pleasure in him."* [39] *But we are not of those who draw back to*

72

perdition, but of those who believe to the saving of the soul."

(Hebrews 10:23, 35-39 NKJV)

> **_Faith is contacted at a point... NOW! not tomorrow, There must be a point... NOW._**

[1]*"Now faith is the substance of things hoped for, the evidence of things not seen.* [2] *For by it the elders obtained a good testimony.* [3]*By faith we understand that the worlds were framed by the word of God, so that the things which are seen were not made of things which are visible.*

[6] *But without faith it is impossible to please him, for he who comes to God must believe that he is, and that he is a rewarder of those who diligently seek him." (Hebrews 11:1-3, 6 NKJV)*

'For I say through the grace given to me, to everyone who is among you, not to think of himself more highly than he ought to think, but to think soberly, as *God has dealt to each one a measure of faith.'* (Romans 12:3 NKJV)

WHAT IS THE POINT OF FAITH? (THE BOILING POINT IN PRAYERS)

From the scriptures above, Hebrews 11:1 says NOW Faith is... The Substance of things hoped for... The Evidence of things not seen!

Faith is contacted at a point... NOW! not tomorrow, There must be a point... NOW.

It is when we lay hold on the Substance, the Evidence, and the Proof of our prayers... Until you see tangible proof of your answers ... you are not in Faith. It is when you get to the Boiling Point in Prayers... The point of Faith... The NOW Faith is!

There is a point in contacting Faith... There is a point you lay holds on the Substance of things you are hoping for, the evidence of the things not yet seen!

HOW AND WHEN DO YOU GET TO THE POINT OF FAITH IN PRAYERS?

To get to the Point of Faith in prayers, the Boiling Point in Prayers, the following three steps would have been set in motion. They are Preparations for Prayers, Clearing your hearing channel, and Hearing the Word of Faith spoken to you.

1. PREPARATIONS FOR PRAYERS...

As already discussed in the earlier chapter... You should have identified the kind of prayers you are engaging in and the level of prayers involved. You should have also identified the Scriptures you are standing on and started brooding on these scriptures; this expected that you are already creating the right atmosphere for GOD and abstinent from all manner of sins...

What is the word of GOD saying about your situation... What is the word of GOD saying about your desire...

Begin to brood on these scriptures, meditating on them, praying them, singing them, reading them out loud, chanting them, checking the meanings of the words, comparing different versions of these scriptures, 'romancing' these scriptures... Waiting on the Word daily as you create an enabling environment for GOD's Glory in your life. When these are in order, you are getting ready to get to the point of Faith.

> **GOD is always speaking; however, many are not hearing because their hearing channel is clogged with thoughts of sins and lawlessness**

2. CLEARING YOUR HEARING CHANNEL...

Another crucial step in attaining the point of faith is clearing your hearing channel. Why do you need this? GOD is always speaking; however, many are not hearing because their hearing channel is clogged with thoughts of sins and lawlessness. In our Book: *'Understanding the works of darkness,'* we dealt extensively with the different devices of the enemy against Christians today. The Force of Distraction is one such device, using Thoughts as its tool.

Thoughts are not just for information; thoughts are an influencing tool; any thought you are not addressing, you are submitting to.

When over 60,000 thoughts flying daily through man's mind are not brought into captivity to obey CHRIST; apart from primarily distracting one from CHRIST and HIS ANOINTING, they also clog the hearing channel, so one does not hear the Spirit of GOD speaking in us. Clogging is a serious job of the wanding thoughts!

This clogging prevents access to the point of Faith. As long as thoughts are not guided in the life of a man praying, such a one will not get to the Boiling Point in his prayers, hence not accessing the Substance of things hoped for and the evidence of things not seen.

Thoughts are not just for information; thoughts are an influencing tool; any thought you are not addressing, you are submitting to.

Romans 10:17 says, 'Faith comes by HEARING, and HEARING by the Word of GOD'. **The Spirit of God must speak the Word of Faith, the Substance of your answer, to you**. It is the major tool for your prayers, which is this Word of FAITH... this is the substance of things you are hoping for, and the evidence of things you are yet to see must be spoken to you... It must be by HEARING...

'So then Faith comes by hearing, and hearing by the word of God.' (Romans 10:17 NKJV).

Faith does not come by just reading the Bible; Faith must be spoken to your spirit… and you are to HEAR it… The Word of GOD is not just the Bible; the Word of GOD is hidden inside the Bible… You have to dig deep to access it. **As you dig deep into the Word of God, your hearing channel is cleared, so you now hear the Word of Faith spoken to your spirit.**

> *Faith does not come by just reading the Bible; Faith must be spoken to your spirit… and you are to HEAR it…*

Thoughts are deliberate counterfeit to the voice of GOD… Hence the need to clear your Hearing Channel off of thoughts to hear the Word of Faith!

HOW DO WE CLEAR OUR HEARING CHANNEL?

As described above, your hearing channel needs to be cleared of thoughts to hear the Word of Faith for your prayers. To clear your hearing channel, first, you must develop the habit and lifestyle of renewing your mind by the Word of GOD… Only the Word of GOD can silence the thoughts of sins flooding man's mind daily. As you subject your mind to the Word of God, your mind aligns with the new information and adapts to the Word. Science call this Neuroplasticity.

'And do not be conformed to this world, but be transformed by the renewing of your mind, that you may prove what is that good and acceptable and perfect will of God.' (Romans 12:2 NKJV)

The second way to clear the hearing channel is by taking no Thoughts. Do not entertain thoughts. Take No Thoughts.

> *As you subject your mind to the Word of God, your mind aligns with the new information and adapts to the Word. Science call this Neuroplasticity.*

Through the Prophet Isaiah, the Spirit of God revealed the mind of GOD concerning thoughts. GOD says 'Speak the word' instead! Our Lord JESUS CHRIST, in one of His sermons, repeatedly said,' Take no Thoughts'... is not just as a piece of advice. Instead, it is a command to be taken seriously and adhere to always!.

When you entertain wandering thoughts, you submit to the lordship of the thought's initiator (Enemy), clogging your hearing channel alongside... (Isaiah 55:8-11: Matthew 6:24-34).

The Spirit of CHRIST is always speaking. However, you may not always hear... Until you clear your hearing channel, you will not

78

hear... **Thoughts are deliberate counterfeit to the voice of GOD...**
The primary mission of wandering thoughts is to clog your hearing
channel. Thus, GOD made it so clear... 'My thoughts are not your
thoughts.' GOD does not dwell on thoughts. He speaks forth... He
creates... and HE created us that way and wants us to operate as
such: Creating instead of giving in to thoughts...

[8] *"<u>For my thoughts are not your thoughts,</u> Nor are your ways My
ways,' says the Lord.* [9] *'For as the heavens are higher than the
earth, So are My ways higher than your ways, And My thoughts
than your thoughts.* [10] *'For as the rain comes down, and the snow
from heaven, And do not return there, But water the earth, And
make it bring forth and bud, That it may give seed to the sower
And bread to the eater,* [11] *<u>So shall My word be that goes forth from
My mouth</u>; it shall not return to Me void, But it shall accomplish
what I please, And it shall prosper in the thing for which I sent it."
(Isaiah 55:8-11 NKJV)*

*'Therefore I say unto you, <u>Take no thought</u> for your life, what ye
shall eat, or what ye shall drink, nor yet for your body, what ye
shall put on. Is not life more than meat, and the body than
raiment? (Matthew 6:25 NKJV)*

Lastly, to clear your hearing channel, the Spirit of God, through
Apostle Paul, urges us to bring every thought into captivity to obey
CHRIST. Now, this is the duty and responsibility of every believer!

Thoughts may not naturally submit to CHRIST, hence the need to bring them into CAPTIVITY... forcefully, by repeatedly and continuously speaking the word of GOD on and against it, until the thoughts submit to the Word.

[3] 'For the weapons of our warfare are not carnal but mighty in God for pulling down strongholds, [4] casting down arguments and every high thing that exalts itself against the knowledge of God, [5] <u>bringing every thought into captivity to the obedience of Christ</u>.' (2 Corinthians 10:3-5 NKJV)

As you speak the scriptures, sing with it, pray with it, meditate on it, study it, wait on it... you are brooding on the Word.., teaching your mind, and arresting thoughts to obey the Word... **Very soon, if you stay long enough on this, the Spirit of Life in the Word will jump out of the scriptures for you. You will hear the same word spoken to you. You will get to the Boiling Point of Faith!**

A journey to battling your mind and bringing all thoughts into submission to CHRIST... This process is done by speaking the word of GOD... in all and at all instances of thoughts. Depending on the state of your mind, this may take a while; however, if you are a regular mind-renewing Christian, it will only take a few moments. Your mind is to be renewed by the word of GOD... You have to teach your mind to agree with the word of GOD... Cancelling every imagination and every high thing that exalts itself against the will of GOD... And bringing all thoughts into captivity to obey CHRIST...

This exercise is where the works come into play... It may take days, weeks, months... However, when you are serious, it should not take that long... That is why, as believers, we habitually wait on the word of GOD so that our mind is in constant renewal ... If your mind is not renewed... You cannot pray in faith!

> **When your mind is not renewed... You cannot pray in faith...**

"and do not be conformed to this world, but be transformed by the renewing of your mind, that you may prove what is that good and acceptable and perfect will of God." (Romans 12:2 NKJV)

Remember that God has dealt with everyone with a measure of faith... Therefore, everyone is operating in faith of some sort. **Faith is neutral... Faith takes on the highest knowledge bidder**... For everyone dished a measure of faith... Your faith is working right now... Taking on your highest knowledge.

'For I say through the grace given to me, to everyone who is among you, not to think of himself more highly than he ought to think, but to think soberly, as <u>God has dealt to each one a measure of faith.</u>' (NKJV). To take on the faith in GOD, you must have evidence... Proof of knowledge of GOD's will on that issue...

So speak the word... Sing the word... Meditate on the word... Cram the word... Chant the word... Brood on the word... Paste it everywhere to see it... Say it repeatedly... Pray it in tongues... until they become your realities!

What you are doing is... Pulling down other knowledge against the Word of God in your mind... And bringing all thoughts to submit to the Word before you... Hence clearing your hearing channel...

> *Faith is neutral... Faith takes on the highest knowledge bidder...*

When your hearing channel is cleared, you will hear CHRIST speak the Word of Life from within you...

This process may take some time... Whatever it takes... Engage it... And you will reap the dividend of the prayers...

This step, clearing your hearing channel, is very important in your journey to effective prayer life. **No matter how many scriptures you know or how long you pray, if the Spirit of God cannot speak the Word of Faith into your Spirit, you will not achieve your desired answers to prayers.**

These evil and clogging thoughts can come in the form of problems, complexities of a situation, hopelessness of the problem and references to people on similar journeys...

82

Moreover, thoughts can also come in the form of your desired results, a fantasy about what you are wishing or praying for, a pseudo comfort that your prayers are answers...

No matter what side of the coin the thoughts pull through, they deliberate counterfeiting the Voice of GOD, and they are gunning to clog your hearing channel, so you might not hear the Spirit of GOD speak the Word of Faith into your Spirit.

The thoughts you do not address, you are submitting to, the content, whether good or bad, notwithstanding. Please always remember that...

Make the Word of GOD a final authority in your life, and in that situation, you are praying on. Speak the Word, in season, and out of season... speak the word, when convenient or not... Speak the word, against all thoughts, whether they sound god or evil... simply say your selected word... until the Word prevail for you.

'Preach the Word! Be ready in season and out of season. Convince, rebuke, exhort, with all longsuffering and teaching.' (2 Timothy 4:2 NKJV).

Let your mind be the very first person you preach to, for if you win your mind over, you will also become a BLESSING to others too. 'Preach the Word!'... Make it a duty; to clear your hearing channel...

3. HEAR THE WORD SPOKEN BY THE SPIRIT OF CHRIST...

For faith comes by HEARING... Not reading... And hearing by the word of GOD...

How do you hear the word of GOD? It must be spoken to you... Not read... Spoken by the Spirit of CHRIST in you... You cannot hear CHRIST... (The Spirit of CHRIST) in you speak If your mind is hearing other things...

"it is the Spirit who gives life; the flesh profits nothing. The words that I speak to you are Spirit, and they are life." (John 6:63 NKJV)

"Who also made us sufficient as ministers of the new covenant, not of the letter but of the Spirit; for the letter kills, but the Spirit gives life." (2 Corinthians 3:6 NKJV)

"And because you are sons, God has sent forth the Spirit of His Son into your hearts, crying out, "Abba, Father!" (Galatians 4:6 NKJV)

It is the Spirit of GOD's Son... In your heart, that speaks ... Abba, Father... The word that GOD hears is the voice of His Son... You must let CHRIST talk from inside of you...

So Begin to read... And read... And read... Until the Holy Spirit speak the word back from within you...

When the mind, thoughts and imaginations are brought to agree with the word of GOD, then the Spirit of GOD living inside of you will speak the word of GOD forth... The Holy Spirit will speak the word of GOD out... through your mouth! Alleluia!

This time... Unlike all these while you have been saying it yourself... This time... When the Spirit of God speaks the word through you... This time, the word becomes Quick, Powerful, Sharper than any two-edged swords... This becomes your substance... And your evidence of things hopes for. This becomes your Faith... The most important tool you need in Prayer...

So Begin to read... And read... And read... Until the Holy Spirit speak the word from within you...

Once your hearing channel is cleared of thoughts, you will hear the WORD OF FAITH... This point is when the Word of GOD becomes LIFE and POWERFUL in your Mouth... Because it will no longer be you speaking it, it will be the Spirit of CHRIST speaking the Word through you.

'for it is not you who speak, but the Spirit of your Father who speaks in you.' (Matthew 10:20 NKJV)

This junction is when you get to the Point of Faith, the Boiling Point in your prayers... The Word of Faith will be spoken to your spirit, and you will HEAR it. This is when the Word of GOD becomes creative, powerful, and sharper than any two-edged sword, ready to fix just about anything spoken of or faced up with.

Just like a boiling point... in the process of boiling water, your preparations must get to this point in prayers... Where the word of GOD you speak, meditate, sing and wait on becomes THE WORD OF FAITH...

> *Once your hearing channel is cleared of thoughts, you will hear the WORD OF FAITH... This point is when the Word of GOD becomes LIFE and POWERFUL in your Mouth... Because it will no longer be you speaking it, it will be the Spirit of CHRIST speaking the Word through you.*

Until you get to this Boiling Point in prayers, you cannot guarantee an answer to your prayers. Many lack this understanding; hence do not push to this point, even in their many years of praying... Getting to the Point of Faith, the Boiling Point in Prayers, is not as much of HOW LONG; instead, it is HOW WELL you pray. You may never get to this point without preparations and clearing your hearing channel. Pause, Ponder, and Think about this!..

This vacuum is one of the reasons why there are few answers to prayers today! We pray for God's Mercies...

Many people quote and believe the scriptures sincerely; however, they do not get to the point of Faith; therefore, the Word does not turn to THE WORD OF FAITH, hence no results to show for it.

Many Christians died quoting the scriptures; many are sick, oppressed, and in dire situations simply because they did not get access to the Word of FAITH at the Boiling Point in Prayers.

These cases ought not to be so, now you know, Take this and begin to apply it in your life situation... Preparations, Clearing your Hearing channel... and endeavour to get to the Boiling Point so that you might access the Word of FAITH. *'For Faith comes by HEARING, and HEARING by the Word of GOD'...* *(Romans 10:17)*

Getting to the Point of Faith, the Boiling Point in Prayers is not as much of HOW LONG; instead, it is HOW WELL you pray

Let us look at these scriptural verses below more closely...

When we pray according to the will of GOD... He hears us...

"Now this is the confidence that we have in him, that if we ask anything according to his will, he hears us. And if we know that he hears us, whatever we ask, we know that we have the petitions that we have asked of him." (1 John 5:14-15 NKJV)

Without faith, it is impossible to please GOD...

"But without faith it is impossible to please him, for he who comes to God must believe that he is, and that he is a rewarder of those who diligently seek him." (Hebrews 11:6 NKJV)

When the son of man comes, will He really find faith on this earth...? Our Lord JESUS CHRIST equated faith to persistence in the place of prayer...

"Then the Lord said, "Hear what the unjust judge said. And shall GOD not avenge his own elect who cry out day and night to Him, though He bears long with them? I tell you that He will avenge them speedily. Nevertheless, when the Son of Man comes, will He really find faith on the earth?" (Luke 18:6-8 NKJV)

Our Lord JESUS CHRIST equates Faith with persistent in prayers ... Not just persistence, it is persistence on the desired outcome, the will of GOD... which is the Word of GOD!

Until you get to this point, you have not prayed... When you get to the Point of Faith... The Boiling Point... You will know that you know that you know that you know... That the Word works...

Once you get to the 'Boiling Point of Faith', you access your Word of Faith, your Proof, your Evidence of Faith, and your Substance of Faith. When you get your Point of Faith... Pray it now... Declare that word of life ... With authority... Within minutes... At that instance... GOD hears... GOD answers... Things change... Doors open... Miracles take place... Healing takes place... etc. This time is when from the above scriptures, 'GOD avenge them speedily'...

WHAT THEN IS FAITH?

The substance of things hoped for... The evidence of things not seen... It is having something tangible on what you believe GOD for...

"Now faith is the substance of things hoped for, the evidence of things not seen." (Hebrews 11:1 NKJV)

Many pray for evidence and proof... GOD says, Pray with evidence and proof...

Many pray for signs and wonders... However, Hebrews 11:1 says... You should pray with the evidence of signs and wonders...

You have not prayed... Until you have evidence and proof of your answers... You are still preparing for prayers until you access your Word of Faith spoken to you... When you HEAR the Word of Faith... This is your 'substance of things hoped for and the 'evidence of things not seen.' This proof is what you will use in your prayer. Do you understand? I pray the Almighty GOD to grant you insight into this in the Name of YESHUA HAMASHIACH (JESUS CHRIST), Amen.

Waooooo... How do you have this evidence...? How do we have this proof? The essential substance in prayers? Romans 10:17 says Faith comes by hearing... and Hearing by the word of GOD...

What is this 'Word of GOD'? The word of GOD is not just the bible... **The Word of God is hidden in the scriptures... Until you dig deep and long enough..., you will not encounter the word of GOD...**

> *Many pray for evidence and proof... GOD says, Pray with evidence and proof...*
>
> *Many pray for signs and wonders... However, Hebrews 11:1 says, You should pray with the evidence of signs and wonders...*

The NOW of the Word of GOD... The 'NOW Faith is'... This is the Word of Life. It is your evidence and proof ... The tool for your prayers... Our Lord JESUS CHRIST says... The word that He speaks... Are Spirit and are life!

"it is the Spirit who gives life; the flesh profits nothing. The words that I speak to you are Spirit, and they are life." (John 6:63 NKJV)

The question is... Have you heard the Word spoken to you? Faith comes only by HEARING...

For the letter kills... The Spirit gives life...

"who also made us sufficient as ministers of the new covenant, not of the letter but of the Spirit; <u>for the letter kills, but the Spirit gives life</u>." (2 Corinthians 3:6 NKJV)

The word of God is quick and powerful... Nothing is hidden from Him... The Word of God can fix anyone and anything. The problem is that few get to HEAR the Word spoken to them, rendering their prayers ineffective. Any prayer you made without the evidence of things hoped for, without the Word of Faith, is empty from the inception. It will not be fruitful.

> *The question is...*
> *Have you heard the Word spoken to you?*
> *. . .*
> *Faith comes only by HEARING...*

"for the word of God is living and powerful, and sharper than any two-edged sword, piercing even to the division of soul and spirit, and of joints and marrow, and is a discerner of the thoughts and intents of the heart. And there is no creature hidden from his sight, but all things are naked and open to the eyes of him to whom we must give account." (Hebrews 4:12-13 NKJV)

Therefore, the question worth asking is, are you actually praying? Many people stop their prayer journey at the preparation stage... And wonder why GOD is not answering them...

For without faith... It is impossible to please GOD... GOD only hears prayers according to His will. Faith is the substance of things hoped for... The evidence of things not seen... Have you gotten your faith...? On that issue? Until then... You have not prayed...

When this understanding becomes clear to you, you will never record any unanswered prayers again in your life.

THE POINT OF FAITH IS NOT SELF–DETERMINED...

Now, a point worth noting is... No man can initiate the Boiling Point, called Point of Faith. You cannot dictate, say, it will take me 4 hours or four days to get to the Boiling Point in my prayers; however, speedily, once your hearing channel is cleared, you will HEAR the Word of Faith spoken to your spirit.

> *Therefore, the question worth asking is, are you actually praying?*
>
> *. . .*
>
> *Many people stop their prayer journey at the preparation stage... And wonder why GOD is not answering them...*

It is why our Lord JESUS CHRIST, in His parable on the Point of Faith, said... Our heavenly Father bears long and yet comes speedily to avenge His own elects...

[6] "Then the Lord said, "Hear what the unjust judge said. [7] And shall GOD not avenge his own elect who cry out day and night to Him, though He bears long with

them? _[8] I tell you that He will avenge them speedily._ Nevertheless, when the Son of Man comes, will He really find faith on the earth?" (Luke 18:6-8 NKJV)

'The bearing long' is while you are still preparing and clearing your hearing channel... once all those are done, Speedily, GOD steps in, and your miracle is born!

Therefore, though the time to the Boiling Point may NOT be self-determined, the commitment to preparations in prayers and clearing your hearing channel can be intensified, as these are the determining factors to your Point of Faith, the Boiling Point in your prayers.

Like boiling water, as long as the heat is on the water, you can be sure that you will eventually get to the Boiling Point... Do you understand? My dear friend... What will you rather do with this information? Have you actually prayed about that situation? Are you really praying? When the Son of Man (Our Lord Jesus Christ) comes... Will He find faith on this earth?

Prayer Dynamics... We pray that the MERCIES OF GOD prevail for us all in our faith journey in the Name of YESHUA HAMASHIACH (JESUS CHRIST), Amen. You may want to read this chapter again slowly to grasp the revelation therein fully. I sincerely pray that you encounter the insight being shared with you today, in the Name of Yeshua Hamashiach (Jesus Christ), Amen.

Your Notes . . .

The Point of Faith: What do you understand by this?

Your Notes . . .

How are you planning to get to the Point of Faith in your Prayers today?

TAKING ACTIONS IN PRAYERS . . .

Prayer Dynamics ...

5.   PRAYER   DYNAMICS: TAKING ACTIONS IN PRAYER...

PRAYER DYNAMICS ... TAKING ACTIONS IN PRAYER...

*A*ll prayer must terminate in action... Prayer is communication...When you make a request to GOD, GOD will speak back to you, giving you an actionable plan to be taken...

TAKING ACTIONS IN PRAYERS...

Prayers are two-way communication. A man speaks to GOD for a request, and GOD responds with the answer. When God wants to answer your prayers, HE gives you an actionable plan that will birth the miraculous. There is God's part and man's part in every miracle. GOD does the supernatural; Man does the natural, thereby naturally birthing the supernatural!

98

WHY ACTIONS IN PRAYERS?

At the creation of Man, GOD Almighty had a purpose, to make Man After His likeness... And to let them have dominion over everything on this earth...

"Then God said, "Let us make man in our image, according to Our likeness; let them have dominion over the fish of the sea, over the birds of the air, and over the cattle, over all the earth and over every creeping thing that creeps on the earth." (Genesis 1:26 NKJV)

All prayer must terminate in action... Prayer is communication... When you make a request to GOD, GOD will speak back to you, giving you an actionable plan to be taken...

This mandate is still in operation today. As long as this earth remains, Man is the Lord of this earth...

"The heaven, even the heavens, are the Lord's; but the earth He has given to the children of men." (Psalms 115:16 NKJV)

Therefore, If the Man is the Lord of this earth... Man must have a final say... Man is the Lord of this earth... Hence, everything must pass through a man... Man has the final say on this earth. Man's words count here on this earth.

To this effect, in Genesis... GOD created the heavens, earth, animals, vegetation and all...Yet GOD brought every creature He made to Adam (the man) to see what Adam would call them, and whatever Adam called them remains their names...

'Out of the ground the Lord God formed every beast of the field and every bird of the air, and brought them to Adam to see what he would call them. <u>And whatever Adam called each living creature, that was its name.</u>' (Genesis 2:19 NKJV).

> **Man has the final say on this earth! Man must be involved in anything that happens to them on this earth. You must participate because it is your call.**

Man has the final say on this earth! Man must be involved in anything that happens to them on this earth. You must participate because it is your call.

Our Lord JESUS CHRIST raised Lazarus from the dead in the book of John, chapter eleven. He called dead Lazarus forth... Yet He said... 'Lose the clothing and let him go'... which is more manageable, raising the dead or losing the robe on him... However, because man must be involved in all miracles on this earth, He does the supernatural and let man do the natural for the completeness of the miracle.

"Now when he had said these things, he cried with a loud voice, "Lazarus, come forth!" And he who had died came out bound hand and foot with graveclothes, and his face was wrapped with a cloth. JESUS said to them, "Loose him, and let him go." (John 11:43-44 NKJV)

The GOD that created all creatures could not HE name them? Our Lord JESUS CHRIST that raised a dead man, Lazarus... Could not He also command the bandages to be loosened from him?

> *GOD does the supernatural; Man does the natural, thereby naturally birthing the supernatural.*

However, for the mandate of GOD for Man to be complete, with every and anything that has to do with man and on this earth... GOD does the supernatural; Man does the natural, thereby naturally birthing the supernatural.

When Adam sinned and lost dominion over the earth, the earth was cursed for his sake...

'Then to Adam He said, 'Because you have heeded the voice of your wife, and have eaten from the tree of which I commanded you, saying, 'You shall not eat of it': 'Cursed is the ground for your sake; In toil you shall eat of it All the days of your life. Both thorns and thistles it shall bring forth for you, And you shall eat the herb of the field." (Genesis 3:17-18 NKJV)

Hence the earth is operating not in its original state right now... This earth is CURSED... This curse is why Abnormalities, Scarcity, delay, unfruitfulness, disobedience to God, labour, toiling, etc., can occur today. The reason why there is so much labour and toiling today... The earth is Cursed; hence, there is a need for supernatural supplies, provisions, sustenance, healings, directions, etc.

Secondly, the fallen angels... **Satan and his cohorts. They hijacked the ruler-ship of this earth from man, hence controlling the elements of this earth... Using these elements against man, instigating men to use the earth against themselves...** who is supposed to be the Lord of this earth... Therefore, there is a need for supernatural interventions for men in all areas of life.

Goodnews, our Lord JESUS CHRIST redeemed man back to the original position of dominion, even better now, as 'Sons of GOD'.

This redemption is what our Lord JESUS CHRIST came for, to restore... Redeeming man from the curse placed on him... And bringing man back to his original position as the Lord of this earth... And placing man to partake of the fullness of GOD in CHRIST JESUS...

To this effect, even though many evil may occur on this earth... Many oppositions and attacks... However, now that we legally have access to the Father, through the remission of our sins by the Blood of our Lord JESUS CHRIST... We can now birth the supernatural ... In the natural... any day and any time.

However, for the supernatural to happen for you, GOD gives you a little work, while HE does the supernatural. GOD works through you to birth the answers because man is still the Lord of the earth.

Call to me, and I will answer you, and show you great and mighty things, which you do not know.' (Jeremiah 33:3 NKJV)

"Most assuredly, I say to you, he who believes in Me, the works that I do he will do also; and greater works than these he will do, because I go to my father." (John 14:12 NKJV)

"But as it is written: "eye has not seen, nor ear heard, nor have entered into the heart of man the things which God has prepared for those who love Him." But God has revealed them to us through His Spirit. For the Spirit searches all things, yes, the deep things of God." (1 Corinthians 2:9-10 NKJV)

That Man has a corresponding action to take in the birth of his answers to prayer is why the scriptures say, 'For Faith without works is dead.'... (James 2:16-26]. Your Faith must lead to work. You must participate in every creation on this earth that has to do with you! *'Thus also faith by itself, if it does not have works, is dead.' (James 2:17 NKJV)*

WHAT ARE THE WORKS IN PRAYERS?

These are effortless actions based on the instructions the Holy Spirit gave when your prayers are heard, when you hit the 'Boiling Point' in Prayers when you encounter substance, evidence and proof of your answer.

GOD does the supernatural; Man does the natural, giving birth to the supernatural in a natural way...

Examples are:

- GOD made the different creatures and brought them to Adam to name them! (Genesis 2:19)

- Our Lord JESUS CHRIST raised the dead Lazarus and asked the men around to loosen the grave clothes on him. (John 11:43-44).

- Young, unskilled David used ordinary stone to kill a seasoned giant Warrior, Goliath! (1 Samuel 17:45-51).

GOD does the supernatural; Man does the natural, giving birth to the supernatural in a natural way... Think about this.

104

IT IS YOUR RESPONSIBILITY TO TAKE ACTION IN PRAYERS...

When GOD replies to your prayer with an actionable plan... It is your responsibility to take this action... It is at this point that your prayer's answers are guaranteed.

If Man refuses to take action at the instant of Faith, the Bible says such a Faith is dead! (James 2:26).

Many people take action before praying. As a matter of fact, many people today use their actions to help GOD... They take action, proving they believe in GOD... NO! You do not take action to prove your Faith... You take action because your Point of Faith says so!

You do not take action to prove your Faith...

You take action because your Point of Faith says so!

These actions are born from the place of prayers, received at the Boiling Point in Prayers and are meant to usher in the supernatural...

NOTE: **THIS WORK IS NOT BEFORE PRAYERS... THIS WORK IS BORN FROM PRAYERS...IT MUST BE ACTIONS TAKEN AFTER YOU HIT THE BOILING POINT IN PRAYERS...**

They are actions based on specific instructions from GOD in prayers...

It is when a simple natural action becomes a channel for the supernatural manifestation.

The difference between a believer's Faith work and others are:

- You work AFTER Prayers, not BEFORE prayer...

- You work based on instructions from Prayers, the Word of GOD.

- You are working from answers... at the Boiling Point in Prayers...

- You are not working based on LABOUR and toiling...

- You are not working to convince GOD that you believe...

- You work because GOD says so, at your point of Faith in prayers...

- You are not working to help GOD move very fast...

- You work because you heard GOD answers your prayers and gave you your miracle passcode...

- You work expecting a MIRACLE, An Answer, An Overflow...

GOD does the supernatural...Man does the Natural...Causing the Supernatural to be manifested in a natural way.

SOME OTHER REASONS WHY WE WORK... IN PRAYERS?

Apart from the main reason that Man is the Lord of this earth, hence must participate in everything that happens to him on this earth, there are other reasons why GOD wants us to contribute to our miracle-making. They are:

I. YOU WORK BECAUSE GOD DOES NOT LIKE LAZY HANDS...

"for even when we were with you, we commanded you this: if anyone will not work, neither shall he eat." (2 Thessalonians 3:10 NKJV).

"Thus also faith by itself, if it does not have works, is dead. But someone will say, "you have faith, and I have works." Show me your faith without your works, and I will show you my faith by my works.

You see then that a man is justified by works, and not by faith only.

For as the body without the Spirit is dead, so faith without works is dead also." (James 2:17-18, 24, 26 NKJV)

II. YOU WORK... SO THAT YOUR MIRACLE MAY LOOK LEGITIMATE HERE ON EARTH...

When you work on your miracle passcode... You have the full barking of heaven... All the Divine resources are available to you... Since you are simply taking action on their instruction...

When you work on your miracle passcode... You become the hands of GOD for signs and wonders... An example, GOD will not print earthly currencies and rain them from heaven for you;

however, He can make you so prosper and highly favoured in a business idea He asked you to do, so it looks as if it's the business that birth the supplies! GOD doing the supernatural and man doing the natural, causing the supernatural to be born naturally!

> *When you work on your 'miracle passcode'... You become the hands of GOD for signs and wonders...*

Through you... GOD's multi-faceted wisdom and supremacy are displayed...

It is, therefore, your responsibility to take steps in line with the received plans.

Our Lord JESUS CHRIST gave the loaves of bread that He has BLESSED to his disciples to share with the people in groups... And the five loaves of bread multiplied in their hands and fed over 5,000 people with an overflow of 12 baskets full of leftovers! This is overflow... That is food for thought...

Follow your nudging of steps to take... They may be outrageous... They may sound too simple and easy. In fact, most of the time, they seem too easy to be true... At this point, you need more courage to step out than anything else... However, it is advisable that once you hit your Boiling Point in Prayers and receive instruction on your miracle passcode, Make steps with speed... Swiftly... Some actions may require some preparation... others may be swiftly...

Some more examples in the scriptures...

Paul and Silas were kept in prison, they prayed and sang ... and a miracle happened, and they took action.

Peter was kept in prison to be killed... The church prayed... GOD heard and sent an angel to the jail, who told Peter, 'Rise quickly...

What are the kinds of actions to be taken?

...

They will be something within your reach...

...

They become a natural channel to birth the supernatural...

And as he obeyed the angel and rose, the prison chains were broken. And prison doors open... Peter took action by obeying the angel to leave the prison swiftly.

As soon as the Holy Spirit reveals to you ... your miracle passcode, take action... What are the kinds of activities to be taken? They will be something within your reach... Easy and Effortless step... And as you take these natural, simple actions... They become the natural channel to birth the supernatural...

My dear friend, what will you rather do with this information?

You can cease from that labour, struggle, toiling, and oppression. Sickness, bondage and affliction, and begin to receive answers to your prayers from today.

If you taste the GOODNESS of GOD once, you will never remain the same. Join the saints that are living in the Sabbath Rest of GOD today. Begin to pray more effectively... and get answers to your prayers...

RETURN TO GIVE GOD ... ALL THE PRAISE...

As you experience the Goodness of GOD in your life, you must return to give GOD all the praise. For as you acknowledge and return to give GOD thanks, HE sees to it that you attract more of HIS GOODNESS. (Mark 4:25).

'For whoever has, to him more will be given; but whoever does not have, even what he has will be taken away from him.' (Mark 4:25 NKJV).

Actions taken based on revelation from God in Prayers are not mere works... They are GOD using your instruments **to work a miracle here on earth...** GOD does the SUPERNATURAL... Man does the NATURAL... Leading to the manifestation of the Supernatural in a Natural way on this earth...

GOD has what to do... Man has what to do... to birth the Answers to your Prayers!

GOD does the supernatural...Man does the natural...To reveal the supernatural in the natural...

GOD does the supernatural... Man does the natural... To display the supernatural in the natural...

Just working will not birth supernatural ...However, when a man contacts heaven... Heaven answers...as the man takes action based on the instruction of heaven...Such a Man will show forth the supernatural in the natural ...Let us pay close attention to this...

Prayer Dynamics... Preparations for Prayers... The Point of Faith... (The Boiling Point of Prayer) and Taking action in Prayers...

My dear friend, what will you rather do with this information?

Your Notes...

Taking Actions in Prayers... Why do you need to take Action in Prayers? And Who directs you on the actions to be taken in Prayers?

Your Notes . . .

When do you take action in prayers? Before, During, After Prayers, or At the Point of Faith? Please explain...

MERCY

CONTINUUM...

Prayer Dynamics ...

6. MERCY CONTINUUM···

WHAT IS MERCY CONTINUUM…

*T*he MERCY CONTINUUM . . . **There is a myth that you ask for GOD's MERCIES only when you are in sins… hence, whenever we feel that we are not doing anything wrong according to our judgement, we dismiss the need for GOD's MERCIES… this is not true!**

We, however, need to understand that the sins accrued to us are in three categories… The Adamic Sinful nature, which we inherit as a default once we are born into this world…

Also is the inherited sins from our past parents, grandparents, great grandparents, till the fourth generation of both our maternal and paternal sides… Even if you know why they committed the sins or not, just as you share their genes, physical resemblance, characters and sickness traits … we also partake of

116

their sins and the consequences of their sins. As a matter of fact, because we partake of their sins, we could share their sin's effects, such as sickness and oppression.

The last category of sins is the Self-acquired sins... The sins you commit yourself, consciously or due to peer pressure or demonic influences... Of all the sins categories, we can control the self-acquired sins to some extent; however, the Adamic sinful nature and the inherited sins of past parents, you cannot control nor stop their consequences... Therefore, the reason why you need to engage the MERCIES OF GOD... even in the face of seemingly right and good character and godliness...

Because of all these sins and their consequences, limitations, stagnations and hindrances are placed in men's lives at different junctions of their lives. This sin debt is why you can see a good man of GOD, yet with a failed marriage, abused life, struggling, etc. Or good Christians have many things wrong with their health!

Another critical reason for GOD's MERCIES is that: At Salvation, the Blood of our Lord JESUS CHRIST paid for all our sins and the consequences of our sins... All of them... However, as with all BLESSINGs we inherit in CHRIST, they are to be enacted and activated by Faith. **Therefore, receiving JESUS CHRIST as your Lord and Saviour does not make you begin PHYSICALLY to enjoy**

all of the benefits of Salvation. You are responsible for searching for what is written about you and receiving them by Faith.

This gap: (The need to enact all BLESSING by Faith) leads to different degrees of compliance, hence have caused many to have manifestations of sins and their consequences such as sicknesses, ill characters, limitations, stagnations, and unexplainable setback, even as Christians.

'...but the just shall live by his faith.' (Habakkuk 2:4b NKJV) ...

If you do not enact these promises by faith, the BLESSING will not manifest in your life. Hence why believers have varying degrees of GOD's BLESSING manifested in them.

The Mercies of GOD spans from towards the SINNERS... manifests at SALVATION... show forth in GROWING UP in Faith... and empowers for REIGNING in GLORY!

This responsibility again is MERCIES GAP... The MERCIES of GOD fill those gaps and the unexplainable sins speaking against the saints.

The Mercies of GOD spans from towards the SINNERS... manifests at SALVATION... show forth in GROWING UP in Faith... and empowers for REIGNING in GLORY!

As a Christian, as long as you are on this earth, you will need to engage THE MERCIES OF GOD… For the MERCIES of GOD spans throughout all the life journey of a man on earth.

In this book, Prayer Dynamics, it pleased the Lord that we include this truth… So that after all you have done, walking in love, acting in Faith, preparing for Prayers, attaining the Point of Faith in Prayers, and taking actions in prayers… It is still vital to engage the MERCIES OF GOD, always…

One day the Spirit of GOD told me, 'As long as you are on this earth, you will need my MERCY to reign'… The Bible talks of the COVENANT of the Sure Mercies of David… He also speaks of MERCIES to overcome the forces of darkness…

'Incline your ear, and come unto me: and your soul shall live; and I will make an everlasting covenant with you, even the sure mercies of David.' (Isaiah 55:3 KJV)

[72]'To perform the mercy promised to our fathers And to remember His holy covenant, [73]The oath which He swore to our Father Abraham: [74]To grant us that we, Being delivered from the hand of our enemies, Might serve Him without fear, [75]In holiness and righteousness before Him all the days of our life.' (Luke 1: 72-75 NKJV).

The Mercies of GOD span from Towards the Sinners at Salvation, to Growing up in Faith and Reigning in Life. This is the Mercy Continuum. Let us take a closer look at them.

I. GOD'S MERCIES TOWARDS SINNERS...

GOD's sovereignty reaches out to all men..., some more than the others... And He shows them mercies. The Bible shows these in the lives of the following women: Tamar, Rahab, Ruth, Syrophoenician woman... etc. Although they were gentiles and alienated from GOD's people at their times. GOD yet brought them into His people's commonwealth of BLESSING, their sins were forgiven, they became listed in the genealogy of the Messiah, and some got their sick healed.

'For He says to Moses, 'I will have mercy on whomever I will have mercy, and I will have compassion on whomever I will have compassion.' (Romans 9:15 NKJV)

Randomly, GOD, in His sovereignty, chooses to have Mercy on anyone, and so be it. For no just cause!

In addition to this random Mercy towards the sinners, today, those whose past parents had loved GOD so dearly & sacrificially..., GOD remembers their children and show them Mercies..., even if these children or children's children are yet to know and love GOD. We see this a lot in the western world, where children of past missionaries or ministers of GOD enjoy some GOODNESS they never participate in creating.

'He has helped His servant Israel, in remembrance of His mercy,' (Luke 1:54 NKJV)

II. GOD'S MERCIES AT SALVATION...

For all have sinned and come short of GOD's Glory, Yet GOD shows His Mercy on all, as many that reach out for it at Salvation.

'For God so loved the world, that He gave His only begotten Son, that whoever believes in Him, should not perish, but have everlasting life.'... (John 3:16 NKJV)

At salvation, all our sins are forgiven us... Self-acquired sins, inherited sins, the default Adamic sinful nature, and their consequences ... All forgiven at salvation...Colossians 1:13-14

[13] *'He has delivered us from the power of darkness and conveyed us into the kingdom of the Son of His love,* [14] *in whom we have redemption through His blood, the forgiveness of sins.' (Colossians 1: 13-14 NKJV)*

We earn this Mercy through the Blood of JESUS... And it is open and available for all men, women, young and old.

Many people can relate to this type of MERCIES… yes, I was a sinner; the Lord had mercy on me, and now I am saved by the Blood of JESUS… However, the MERCY of GOD is beyond Salvation… Let us see more below…

III. GOD'S MERCIES FOR GROWING UP…

In Christianity… GOD expects us to forsake our old life and embrace the nature of CHRIST in righteousness and holiness. This process, however, is not automatic… We pass through the rising and falling stages until we can stand sure…

[8] *'If we say that we have no sin, we deceive ourselves, and the truth is not in us.* [9]*If we confess our sins, He is faithful and just to forgive us our sins and to cleanse us from all unrighteousness.* [10]*If we say that we have not sinned, we make Him a liar, and His word is not in us.' (1 John 1:8-10)*

'My little children, these things I write to you, so that you may not sin. And if anyone sins, we have an Advocate with the Father, Jesus Christ the righteous. [2]*And He Himself is the propitiation for our sins, and not for ours only but also for the whole world.' (1 John 2:1-2)*

The MERCIES of GOD caters to the sins of the believers growing up. What a MERCIFUL GOD we serve!

The mercies of GOD show forth at this junction... And as we embrace this Mercy..., we obtain Grace to become strong... How do we access this GRACE ... Let us see a secret from the scriptures here...

[15]*'For we do not have a High Priest who cannot sympathize with our weaknesses, but was in all points tempted as we are, yet without sins. [16]Let us therefore come boldly to the throne of grace, that we may obtain mercy and find grace to help in time of need.'* (Hebrews 4:15-16 NKJV)

As believers grow up, the Lord repeatedly caters to this season of rising and falling into sins. He gave a way of escape, lest Satan should take advantage of us.

Whenever you fall into sin, no matter how small or big the sin is, and you go to God to say 'Father, I am sorry'... genuinely, not proudly, you obtain Mercies... and just before you leave, GRACE is also poured unto you... and you become stronger to withstand and war against the sin.

Many believers have taken this great way of escape for granted and simply forget to repent and say, 'I am sorry.' When you seek GOD's MERCY, that is your passcode to entering the Throne of Grace for GRACE! When you do not repent and say I am sorry for any and all sins, you open yourself to the entrance of the darkness, and you block the opportunity to receive GRACE to help you against the easily enslaving sins. **Think about this...**

'MERCY is your passcode to the Throne of Grace, where GRACE is dispensed as needed!

When you sin as a Christian, it is a stain on your spiritual garment and a sure entrance to the forces of darkness. It is why GOD make this MERCY available for your growing up. This Mercy empowers the believer to live right in righteousness. This Mercy also helps you to show mercies towards others, having tasted the Goodness of GOD... This MERCY enables you to be merciful and deal with other people more tenderly and mercifully.

'Blessed are the merciful, For they shall obtain mercy.' (Matthew 5:7 NKJV)

'For judgement is without mercy to the one who has shown no mercy. Mercy triumphs over judgement.' (James 2:13 NKJV)

IV. GOD'S MERCIES FOR REIGNING!..

And very importantly, as a man on this earth, we may not be able to access the fullness of CHRIST's Grace without the Mercies of GOD...

When Moses asked GOD to show him, His glory..., GOD responded that He would have compassion (mercy) on whom He chooses! It took the MERCIES of GOD to partake in this kind of Divine connectivity.

[18]'*And he (Moses) said, I beseech thee, shew me thy glory*' [19]*Then He (GOD) said, 'I will make all my goodness pass before thee, and*

> **We cannot enjoy the fullness of GOD without the MERCIES of GOD while we are on this earth.**

I will proclaim the name of the Lord before thee, and I will be gracious to whom I will be gracious, and I will shew mercy on whom I will shew mercy.' (Exodus 33:18-19 KJV)

One day, the Spirit of God opened my eyes to this scripture: '*… and I will proclaim the name of the Lord before thee.*'

What? GOD proclaiming His Name? I was intrigued… What is the Name of GOD that HE was proclaiming for His Glory to show forth towards Moses…?

In a trance, in the Mercies of God, I saw myself, as it were, participating in that vision. The Spirit of God took me to follow on to the 'next day,' and went to the mountain where Moses was hidden and heard GOD proclaimed His name…

[4] '*So he cut two tablets of stone like the first ones. Then Moses rose early in the morning and went up Mount Sinai, as the Lord had commanded him, and he took in his hand, the two tablets of stone.*

⁵Now the Lord descended in the cloud and stood with him there, and proclaimed the name of the Lord.

⁶And the Lord passed before him and proclaimed, 'The Lord, the Lord God, <u>merciful</u> and gracious, longsuffering, and abounding in goodness and truth, ⁷<u>keeping mercy for thousands, forgiving iniquity and transgression and sin</u>, by no means clearing the guilty, visiting the iniquity of the fathers upon the children and the children's children to the third and fourth generation.' (Exodus 34: 5-7 NKJV)

Think about this... the Name of the Lord is MERCIFUL... May HIS MERCY prevail for your Christian journey in the Name of YESHUA HAMASHIACH (JESUS CHRIST), Amen.

Apostle Paul also testifies that in ministry, as he has received mercies..., he faints not! He was highly conscious of the place of MERCIES all through his ministry.

'Therefore, since we have this ministry, as we have received mercy, we faint not.' (2 Corinthians 4:1 KJV)

Apostle Paul who was notorious for supporting killings and all manner of evil against the church, says in a place... 'I do no man no wrong'... Really? This redemption could only have been possible because of the MERCIES he received for ministry.

'So Paul said, 'I stand at Caeser's judgement seat, where I ought to be judged. To the Jews I have done no wrong, as you very well know.'' (Acts 25:10 NKJV)

Jude 1:2 says MERCIES be multiplied unto you. *'Mercy unto you, and peace, and love, be multiplied.' (Jude 1:2 NKJV).*

> **You cannot go wrong when you call on the MERCIES of GOD. To reign on this earth, you must partake of the MERCIES of GOD... Let this be your everyday prayer...**

Romans 4:13 and 16 revealed a deep secret that everything is of Faith so that it might be by GRACE...

[13]'For the promise that he would be the heir of the world was not to Abraham or to his seed through the law, but through the righteousness of faith. [16]Therefore it is of faith that it might be according to grace, so that the promise might be sure to all the seed, not only to those who are of the law, but also to those who are of the faith of Abraham, who is the father of us all.' (Romans 4:13, 16, NKJV).

Therefore, to partake in any of the BLESSING of Abraham, including the MERCY CONTINUUM, you must receive it by Faith. GOD is not a respecter of person; He is a respecter of Faith.

That means if you do not align with the benefits in the scriptures through faith, you will fall short any day, any time. Could it be why many are falling short of GOD's BLESSINGS? Regardless of how long you are in church, notwithstanding your church's status and title. For as long as you are not in faith, you cannot partake! GOD is not a respecter of person; HE is a respecter of faith!

There is also a hanging Mercy of GOD called THE SURE MERCIES OF DAVID... available for as many as will incline and hear, and align by Faith to the will of GOD...

This mercy is endowed through the active engagement of GOD's presence, among other things. We primarily access this through the Blood of JESUS CHRIST.

> **The Mercy of GOD may be the significant difference in the ease of achievements in some believers' lives and struggles in others'.**

'And in mercy shall the throne be established: and he shall sit upon it in truth in the tabernacle of David, judging, and seeking judgement, and hasting righteousness.' (Isaiah 16:5 KJV)

'Incline your ear, and come to Me. Hear, and your soul shall live; And I will make an everlasting covenant with you- The **sure mercies of David.**' (Isaiah 55:3 NKJV)

We cannot enjoy the fullness of GOD without the MERCIES of GOD while we are on this earth. The Mercy of GOD may be the significant difference in the ease of achievements in some believers' lives and struggles in others'. This MERCY is available; however, it will not be endowed without a faith activation.

GOD Almighty testify of Himself as one that *'keeps mercies for thousands, forgiving their iniquities, transgression and sins...'* *(Exodus 34:6)*

You cannot go wrong when you call on the Mercies of GOD... There is Truth in walking in Holiness, in walking in Faith, in living right and so on... Go also with MERCY... Obtain Mercies, so you faint not... Let Mercies unto you be multiplied in the Name of YESHUA HAMASHIACH (JESUS CHRIST), Amen.

As GOD cause all to be by faith so that we all might partake in His Grace & BLESSING ... Man will always fall short... While on this earth! That is where the Mercies of GOD comes in...

Will you rather embrace this great Grace and make it your companion in this world? You can never get it wrong with the Mercies of GOD! The 'Sure Mercies of David' is available for your take today! ... (Isaiah 55:3)

HOW DO YOU PARTAKE IN THESE MERCIES?

- For Sinner... there is nothing you can do about it. GOD just choose to have mercy on whomever He chooses in His sovereignty.

- At Salvation ... It is the Blood of JESUS CHRIST that qualifies you. You must receive it by Faith as you call on the Name of our Lord JESUS CHRIST...

- For growing up in Faith... As you take the bold step to go and confess your sins regularly, the Lord is faithful and just to forgive you all your sins... and cleanse you from all unrighteousness... He also gives Grace to you, so you become stronger against the sins... and overcome them.

> *Because every BLESSING must be activated by Faith, men will always fall short...*
> *Let the MERCIES OF GOD make up for that gap.*
> *Call on the MERCIES OF GOD DAILY...*

- For reigning in life... When you give yourself up in service to God, loving GOD sacrificially, and asking in faith, you qualify for MERCY.

You cannot go wrong when you call on the MERCIES of GOD. **To reign on this earth, you must partake of the MERCIES of GOD... Let this be your everyday prayer...** especially if you are facing stubborn circumstances in life... Because every BLESSING must be activated by Faith, men will always fall short... Let the MERCIES OF GOD make up for that gap. Call on the MERCIES OF GOD DAILY...

I HAVE MERCIES... I OBTAIN MERCIES, IN THE NAME OF JESUS CHRIST, AMEN.

I HAVE MERCIES... I OBTAIN MERCIES, IN THE NAME OF JESUS CHRIST, AMEN.

I HAVE MERCIES... I OBTAIN MERCIES, IN THE NAME OF JESUS CHRIST, AMEN.

ENGAGING THE MERCIES OF GOD AS A WEAPON ...

The MERCIES of GOD is a great weapon of warfare that every believer must learn about and engage in regularly for ease and smooth running in life. As explained above, as long as every BLESSING of GOD must be activated by faith, many will fall short of them. This gap is why we see a lot of Christians; tongue-talking church-goers and tithe-payers with sickness, oppression, pain, and lack.

> *For long-standing, unexplainable, 'prayer-defiling' problems and issues in believers' lives, there must be a sin, disobedience, a wandering thought or ignorance that the enemy uses as an anchor to buffet such a one.*

For the enemy to effectively gain access to any man's life, health, family, career, business, properties, etc.., there must be an anchor of darkness in and around such a one. The enemy does not operate outside of the darkness. To buffet anyone, such a one must first be dragged under the 'canopy of darkness,' only then can satan have legal access into their lives and all that is theirs.

For the long-standing, persistent, unexplainable, 'prayer-defiling' problems and issues in believers' lives, there must be a sin, unforgiveness, disobedience, a wandering thought or ignorance that the enemy uses as an anchor to buffet such a one.

As long as these 'anchors' are in place, no amount of prayers will matter. These anchors will limit the manifestations of the Most High in such life.

'Yea, they turned back and tempted God, and limited the Holy One of Isreal.' (Psalms 78:41 KJV).

Let us look at these five main 'anchors' the enemy commonly uses to gain access and continue accessing man's life.

THE ANCHOR OF SIN...

Though hands join in hands, a sinner will not go unpunished. For the soul that sins shall die. Sin is Satan's 'SOS.' Sin is a sure entrance of darkness into a man's life. As long as you accommodate sins of any kind in your life, Satan can, through that sin, enter into your life to buffet you continually. He will use such sin as an anchor for persistent sickness, oppression, reproach or lack. You may have to check for such sins today, repent of them, and take cover under the Blood of JESUS.

THE ANCHOR OF UNFORGIVENESS...

Although unforgiveness is a sin, this singular sin is notorious as an 'anchor of darkness' to buffet believers; hence we are highlighting it. Many today are in that continuous oppression of the darkness simply because they hold grudges against someone that hurts them and refuses to forgive them. In our book... *'Understanding the works of darkness'*... the Spirit of GOD revealed to us that 'Strife is a setup against you... irrespective of who and why the strife.' The Bible made it clear that if you do not forgive those who have trespassed against you, neither will your Father in heaven forgives you.

Bitterness and unforgiveness hinder prayers, give satan a chance to use the victims as agents against others and open doors unto the darkness. Unforgiveness is a sure 'anchor' the enemy uses to oppress and afflict many today consistently. See details on how to manage unforgiveness in our [2]book stated above.

---

[2] Understanding the works of darkness...

THE ANCHOR OF DISOBEDIENCE...

As a minister or a responsible child of GOD, The Spirit of GOD leads and guides us in steps and ways to go. We are expected to follow and obey the Holy Spirit's instructions. *'For as many as are led by the Spirit of God, these are sons of God.' (Romans 8:14 NKJV).* As we move unto maturity in Christianity, the Spirit of GOD expects us to learn how to hear and be led by Him. Disobedience to the Spirit of GOD's leading could set one up for the entrance of darkness.

Anytime you disobey the leading of GOD, you are opening yourself up to the danger of darkness' invasion. This disobedience could be a simple day-to-day instruction or a significant leading to something big in your life or ministry. Disobedience is a sure anchor of the enemy to buffet man continually. When you disobey, the Spirit of God is silenced in you.

THE ANCHOR OF WANDERING THOUGHTS...

As we have learnt from previous chapters, Thoughts are not just for mere information, thoughts are tools of influence, and the thought you do not address, you are submitting to. When you expose yourself to wandering thoughts unattended to, as in not rebuking and bringing them into captivity to obey CHRIST (The Word of GOD) in your life, you are exposing yourself to the danger of darkness' invasion. Wandering thoughts can become an anchor the enemy uses to oppress you continuously.

THE ANCHOR OF IGNORANCE...

Ignorance is one of the subtle anchors of darkness against believers. Due to the lack of commitment of many to studying the scriptures and waiting on GOD for spiritual intelligence, they fall short of BLESSING.

> *The Kingdom of CHRIST is governed by rules... Ignorance of these rules is not an excuse... What you do not know will still speak and work against you. This gap is why engaging the Mercies of GOD is key to a victorious Christian life.*

The Kingdom of CHRIST is governed by rules... Ignorance of these rules is not an excuse... What you do not know can and will still speak and work against you.

Many believers suffer today because the enemy uses their ignorance as an anchor to steal, kill, and destroy them, if possible. **This gap is why engaging the Mercies of GOD is key to a victorious Christian life.**

It is essential to avail yourself of the knowledge of who you are in CHRIST JESUS. A lot depends on this knowledge. The Kingdom of CHRIST is governed by rules or principles; ignorance of these rules is not an excuse. What you do not know will still speak and work against you any day and any time! My dear friend, what will you rather do with this information?

HOW TO ENGAGE THE MERCIES OF GOD AS A WEAPON…

Through our Lord JESUS CHRIST, we all have access to the forgiveness of our sins. This MERCY, through the Blood of JESUS, will dissolve any kind of anchor the enemy is hanging on to, to buffet you. As the scriptures say:

'In that day, says the Lord of hosts, 'the peg that is fastened in the secure place will be removed and be cut down and fall, and the burden that was on it will be cut off; for the Lord has spoken.' (Isaiah 22:25 NKJV).

Through the Blood of JESUS, wherein we gain the forgiveness of our sins, Thus fulfilling the above scripture. However, as with every other promise, until you activate this MERCY by faith, the Anchors *(Pegs fastened to a secure place)* will not be removed.

This MERCY is available the day you received JESUS CHRIST as your Lord and Saviour. It launches you into Christianity and keeps you holy and without blame before the Father, in love, all through your journey in life. However, if the enemy perceives your ignorance about this, they will take advantage of it. Therefore, engaging the MERCIES of forgiveness of sins, through the Blood of JESUS, will dissolve and remove every Anchor of Sins, Disobedience, Wandering Thoughts or Ignorance that the force of darkness is using to buffet you persistently.

'In Him we have redemption through His blood, the forgiveness of sins, according to the riches of His grace.' (Ephesians 1:7 NKJV)

'He has delivered us from the power of darkness and conveyed us into the kingdom of the Son of His love, in whom we have redemption through His blood, the forgiveness of sins.' (Colossians 1:13-14 NKJV)

[13]'And you, being dead in your trespasses and uncircumcision of your flesh, He has made alive together with Him, having forgiven you all trespasses, [14]having wiped out the handwriting of requirements that was against us, which was contrary to us. And He has taken it out of the way, having nailed it to the cross. [15]Having disarmed principalities and powers, He made a public spectacle of them, triumphing over them in it.' (Colossians 2:13-15 NKJV)

Stand your ground, repent of any trace of sin, disobedience and wandering thoughts. Engage the BLOOD OF JESUS CHRIST for MERCIES... And all the Anchors will be dissolved. Amen.

You can say this prayer below out loud and mean it until it becomes so real to you.

You Anchors of Sins, Unforgiveness, Disobedience, Wandering Thoughts and Ignorance the enemy is using to oppress me continuously; today, I receive Forgiveness and nullify such anchors through the BLOOD of JESUS CHRIST, in the Name of JESUS, Amen.

Remember, you need to do this until every thought is brought into captivity to obey CHRIST... Insisting on the forgiveness you received through the Blood of JESUS, even in the face of raging opposing circumstances. When you understand this and address these anchors consciously, they will be nullified, and Satan and his cohorts will not have anything to hold on to against you.

Now, thanks be unto God, which always causeth us to triumph in Christ, and maketh manifest the savour of his knowledge by us in every place.' (2 Corinthians 2:14 KJV).

May this scripture always find fulfilment in your life in the Name of YESHUA HAMASHIACH (JESUS CHRIST), Amen. May you enjoy the fullness of GOD's MERCIES in your life and family in the Name of YESHUA HAMASHIACH (JESUS CHRIST), Amen.

'Mercy unto you, and peace, and love, be multiplied'... (Jude 1:2 KJV).

I have Mercies... I obtain GOD's Mercies...through our Lord, JESUS CHRIST... Amen.

Your Notes . . .

The MERCY CONTINUUM... What new thing did you gain from this chapter today?

Your Notes . . .

When do you need to engage the MERCIES of GOD, and Why?

Your Notes . . .

How will you engage the MERCIES of GOD as a WEAPON against long-standing, persistent, troubling problems?

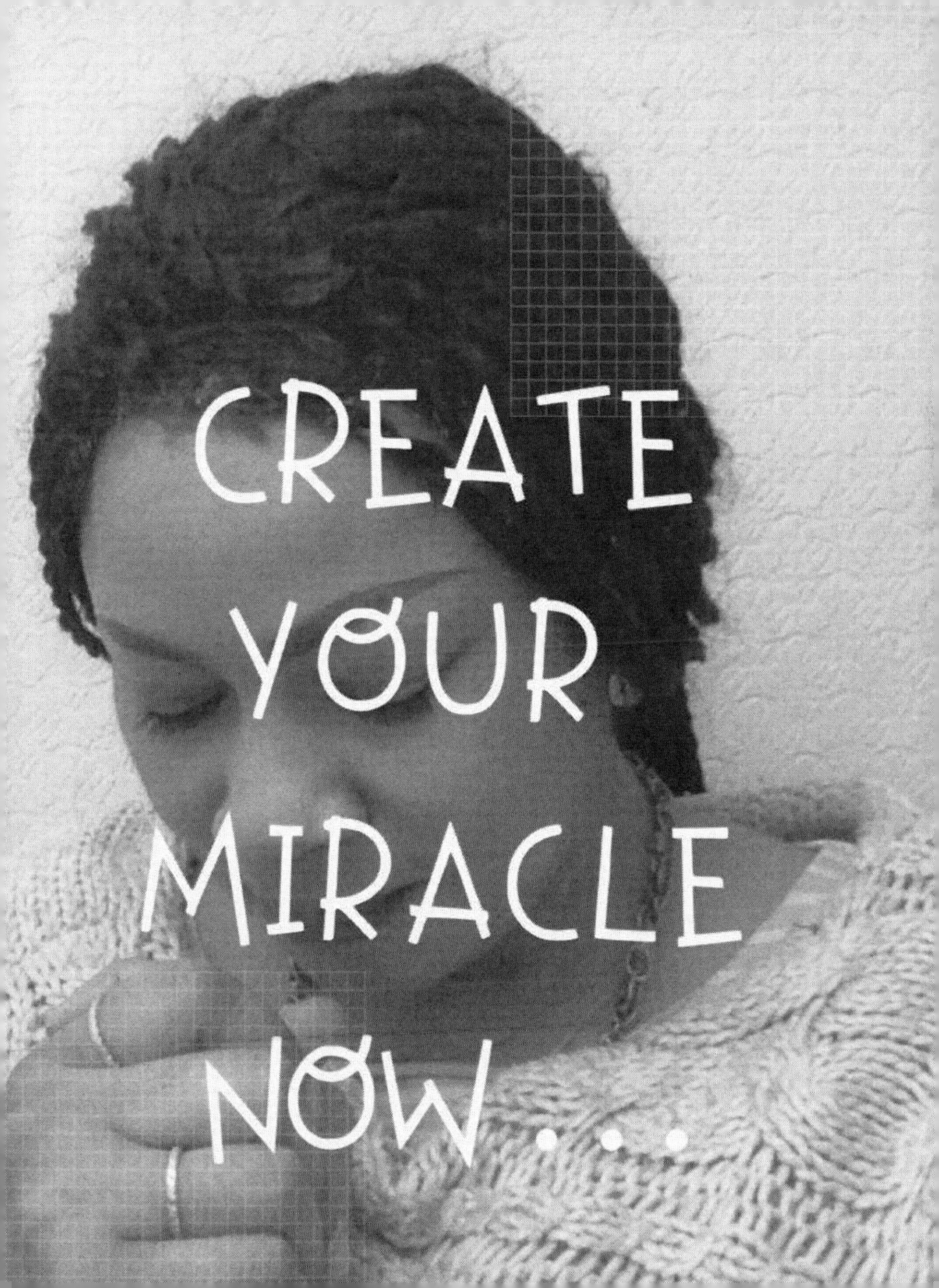
CREATE
YOUR
MIRACLE
NOW...

Prayer Dynamics ...

7. CREATE YOUR MIRACLE··· NOW!

BACKGROUND OF CREATE YOUR MIRACLES ... NOW!

Some years ago, the Spirit of God began to deal with me concerning one of the Gifts of the Spirit... -The Working of Miracles....' As much as in GOD's Mercies, I have seen many of the Divine Gifts of the Spirit operate in and through me; the word choice for this particular one was very intriguing to me... 'The working of Miracles.' It was not until the insights into 'Create your miracle...Now' came that it was getting clearer to me... 'The working of Miracles'...

4'There are diversities of gifts, but the same Spirit. 5there are differences of ministries, but the same Lord. 6And there are

144

diversities of activities, but it is the same God who works all in all. [7]But the manifestation of the Spirit is given to each one for the profit of all: [8]for to one is given the word of wisdom through the Spirit, to another the word of knowledge through the same Spirit. [9]to another faith by the same Spirit, to another gifts of healings by the same Spirit, [10]<u>to another the working of miracles,</u> to another prophesy, to another discerning of spirits, to another different kinds of tongues, to another the interpretation of tongues. [11]But one and the same Spirit works all these things, distributing to each one individually as He wills.' (1 Corinthians 12:4-11 NKJV)

While pondering this great Blessing, I met with two great men of God, my Fathers in the Lord, [3]Brother Kenneth E. Hagin, in his message... 'How to write your own ticket with GOD'. He spoke of his encounter with our Lord JESUS CHRIST on a secret of multiplication... hidden from many; using the Woman with the issue of blood as a case study... it is on YouTube and everywhere.

More recently, I met this great Man of GOD named Br. Gary Keesee, through his book, 'The Money Mysteries from the Master' and some of his other messages...

They BLESSED me immensely; thank you, Sirs. I had been privy to these insights, which I know and have seen work in my life

---

[3] Br. Kenneth E. Hagin, Rhema Bible Church, USA www.rhema.org

severally. However, I do not always see their impact because, when they worked for me, all the secret elements were in place; because I did not know these elements clearly, I often omit some of them and record failure in creating miracles.

From [4]Brother Gary Keesee's teachings, I saw these elements clearly... And I will love to share them with you today...

This is GOD's FAVOUR, ITS A BLESSING, Our GOD is GOOD, and HIS MERCIES endure forevermore, Amen.

These Great men BLESSED me immensely. They gave me confidence that whatever the Spirit of the Lord was revealing to me in this wise is not new to the Church; it is being exposed to many in the church and BLESSING them. Br Gary Keesee has many books on this principle and runs a TV show titled 'Fixing the money thing'... This show is indeed a BLESSING... I stand on the shoulders of these great fathers and all fathers and mothers in the Lord to share this secret with you today...

Our scriptural references are:

'Call to Me, and I will answer you, and show you great and mighty things, which you do not know.' (Jeremiah 33:3 NKJV)

---

[4] Br. Gary Keesee, Life Now Church, Ohio. www.garykeesee.com

"Most assuredly, I say to you, he who believes in Me, the works that I do he will do also; and greater works than these he will do, because I go to My Father." (John 14:12 NKJV)

"But as it is written: "Eye has not seen, nor ear heard, Nor have entered into the heart of man The things which God has prepared for those who love Him." But God has revealed them to us through His Spirit. For the Spirit searches all things, yes, the deep things of God." (I Corinthians 2:9-10 NKJV).

Specifically, our Lord JESUS CHRIST, in all His miracles, reveals this principle's elements. It was expressly and clearly seen on account of His using a small boy's lunch of five loaves and two fish to feed over 5,000 people, as stated in the Gospels: (Matthew 14: 14-21; Mark 6: 34-44; Luke 9: 10-17; and John 6:1-14)

WHY CREATE YOUR MIRACLES...NOW?

The kingdom of CHRIST is governed by rules, which are to be observed to function and effectively reign therein. These laws of the Spirit of Life in CHRIST JESUS supersede all laws, regulations, might, dominion, and all names, now or in the world to come.

GOD urges us to seek this New Kingdom, know how it operates, and discover its righteousness so that supernatural occurrences, signs, wonders and miracles become normal in our lives...

'But seek first the Kingdom of God and His righteousness, and all these things shall be added to you.' (Matthew 6:33 NKJV)

The kingdom of this world began many years ago when GOD created Adam and Eve in the Garden of Eden. (According to the Bible history). However, the present Kingdom of the world was not the initial intended one. The current world is under a proclaimed CURSE as stated in Genesis 3:17-19 when Adam committed treason and fell short of the Glory of GOD. As this was not the original plan of GOD, Plans were set in motion to restore the Kingdom to its original status... The BLESSED Kingdom stated in Genesis 1:22 and 26, 'Be fruitful, multiply, replenish and fill the earth; with Man, having dominion over all of the earth! ... is the Kingdom of CHRIST.

The perverted and cursed kingdom is where we now live and grow up; it shapes our mindset and ways of life. When we willingly submit our lives to JESUS CHRIST, we are transmitted into the invisible New Kingdom, The Kingdom of CHRIST, where things operate according to the order of GOD's BLESSING. This New Kingdom, though invisible, supersedes the present perverted and cursed physical kingdom. Therefore, anyone operating the laws of the Kingdom of CHRIST will live beyond this world's present perverted and cursed kingdom.

Although many of us are born again and now legally brought into the Kingdom of CHRIST, our realities still reflect the old perverted and cursed kingdom of this world where there are sins, lack, oppression, sickness, and labour. This is an ABNORMALITY... Pause, Ponder, and think about this!

Lack of knowledge of the Kingdom of CHRIST that we are bought and brought into is the reason for many oppression today. Hence, believers are in lack, sickness, oppression, and constant labour like others who do not know GOD nor are in the Kingdom of CHRIST...

In this chapter, CREATE YOUR MIRACLE... NOW! We will be looking into the benefits of living in the Kingdom of CHRIST, such as the ability to create miracles... GOD desires to give us His Kingdom; however, He urges us to seek and get to know its righteousness and how it operates. In so doing, we will discover that what the present world people are struggling for, running after, and musing about will become a regular, effortless occurrence in our lives...

Such laws of the Kingdom of CHRIST are the ability to create your life as you go. How do you want it, then create it! This ability is exclusive to the Kingdom of CHRIST and is void of the curses and perversion of Satan and his cohorts.

However, since we Christians are physically living in this world system with all the laid down rules, regulations, and systems, it is vital to learn how the Kingdom of CHRIST operates within it all and begin to apply its principles for our benefit.

The occurrences in the Kingdom of CHRIST are called Miracles in this world system; however, they are simply the normal way of life in the Kingdom of CHRIST...

THE KINGDOM OF CHRIST OPERATES BY RULES

The kingdom of CHRIST is governed by rules, which are to be observed to function and effectively reign therein. These laws of the Spirit of Life in CHRIST JESUS supersede all laws, regulations, might, dominion, and all names, now or in the world to come.

> *The Kingdom of CHRIST operates by CREATION...*
>
> *...*
>
> *You CREATE things, DECREE things, BIRTH things, and live your creation!*

The Kingdom of CHRIST operates by CREATION... You CREATE things; You DECREE things; you BIRTH things, and live your creation.

BLESSING operates in this Kingdom, CHRIST rules in this Kingdom, Sins, Sickness, Oppression, and Lack do not have a place here, and The Forces of Darkness do not understand its existence, let alone oppose it. You bought into this Kingdom when you gave your life to JESUS.

In this chapter, we will be looking into some key elements in creating miracles in the kingdom of CHRIST.

1. What do you have?

2. Name your sample ...

3. Change the kingdom into CHRIST's...

4. Agree with GOD...

5. Release your sample...

6. Harvest your miracle passcode...

7. Harvest your miracles...

Your complete understanding of these elements, how they are to be applied, the GOD's part, your part and the expected outcome will all be spelt out so that beginning from today, you can live in the overflow of GOD despite the evil and the cursed world we live in today. **Let's dig into this...**

The seven steps are for ease of explanations and teaching so we can get the steps. Many of us use these kingdom principles and create miracles; however, because they do not know how it happened, they could not replicate it again and again.

This principle of the Kingdom of CHRIST can be engaged for any and all situations and circumstances irrespective of their degree of wholeness or brokenness... For with God, all things are possible. If you can believe, nothing will be impossible for you.

'Jesus said to him, 'If you can believe, all things are possible to him who believes.' (Mark 9:23 NKJV)

'For with God nothing will be impossible.' (Luke 1:37 NKJV)

If you dare to believe... this principle will work for you any day, time, or situation. Therefore, let us see the seven steps or elements to creating your miracles now... We pray it BLESSES you in the Name of YESHUA HAMASHIACH (JESUS CHRIST), Amen.

CREATE YOUR MIRACLE ... NOW! (1 OF 7)... WHAT DO YOU HAVE?

Do you know that you have something right now that you can use to create your miracle? Everyone has something that can be used to begin the journey to their miracle... Do you know that your MIRACLE is hidden . . . for your good? Do you know that you can CREATE that so much-needed MIRACLE . . . NOW? Why are not many experiencing miracles as of old in the Bible days?

WHAT DO YOU HAVE?

You have something right now that you can use to create your miracle. Everyone has something that can be used to begin the journey to our miracle... Our Lord JESUS CHRIST in Mark 6:38,

152

wanting to create a miracle of feeding thousands of people, asked the disciples... go and see how many loaves you have... In 2 Kings 4: 2, Elisha requested a prophet's widow in need of a miracle ... what do you have in your house? David, in a bit, to defend Israel from their enemies in 1 Samuel 17: 40, had five smooth stones ... to work with!

The woman with the issue of blood in Mark 5: 28 ... says, ' If only I may touch JESUS's garment'... The prodigal son in Luke 15:19 says... 'I will become a hired servant' in my father's vineyard...

My dear friend,   WHAT DO YOU HAVE? There is something about what you have... Everybody has something.   You   have something available to you right now that you can use to start the journey of creating your miracle.

You have something right now that you can use to create your miracle.

Everyone has something that can be used to begin the journey to their miracle...

THE MYSTERY BEHIND WHAT YOU HAVE...

Genesis 1:11 revealed a mandate given by GOD to the earth. Everything on this earth has SEED in it... EVERYTHING... There is a seed of multiplication in everything on the planet, be it machinery, material, skill, ability, money ... ANYTHING and EVERYTHING on this earth has the seed of proliferation. Therefore, what you have has the ability to reproduce and multiply!

'Then God said, 'Let the earth bring forth grass, the herb that yields seed, and the fruit tree that yields fruit according to its kind, whose seed is in itself, on the earth'; and it was so.' (Genesis 1:11 NKJV)

THE CHARACTERISTICS OF WHAT YOU HAVE... (YOUR SAMPLE)

It is available to you right now...

It is the value you place on your miracle...

It is valuable to you...

It is individual-specific...

Is it available to you...

Your Sample can be a material element, a Skill, a Service, an ability, or Money... Money is the most common sample because money is used to value or price many things in the world today and is readily available to everyone. The quantity notwithstanding!

What do you have that can be used to kick-start your journey to creating your miracle? Go and look around you and identify your Miracle sample.

154

Your Notes. . .

PRACTISING - WHAT DO YOU HAVE…

Identify something of value to you, something readily available, Something of value and worth to you, for your miracle today. Set it aside, now. It could be a service, an ability, a skill, service at church, a material such as properties, vehicles, etc., or money.

Identify your sample and write it down here…

CREATING YOUR MIRACLE... NOW! (2 OF 7)... NAME YOUR SAMPLE!

John 14:12 says, 'He that believes in Me, (JESUS CHRIST), the works that I do he will do also, and greater works than these he will do.'... You are empowered in CHRIST to create the desired miracles in your life...

> *Now that you have your Sample, CALL it exactly what you want to see!.*
>
> *It is the responsibility of MAN to name things on earth… You are already naming your world now.*

However, creating miracles answers to Spiritual Law... and it is your knowing this law and how to apply it that causes it to work for you. What are the elements of this law? Why are not many experiencing miracles as in the Bible days?

NAME YOUR SAMPLE . . .

Now that you have your Sample, it is crucial to CALL it exactly what you want it to be. This step is very vital in creating a miracle. God gave man the ability to NAME all the things on this earth.

'Out of the ground the Lord God formed every beast of the field and every bird of the air, and brought them to Adam to see what

he would call them, <u>and whatever Adam called each living</u> <u>creature, that was its name</u>.' (Genesis 2:19 NKJV)

It is a secret, a spiritual ability to be the one to decide what happens on this earth. An essential step in creating your miracle now is to name your sample.

Take your time. Go all the way, as far as real and believable for you! Call it what you want it to be. GOD put all things under man's dominion and control (feet). (Hebrews 2:8), therefore name it as you so wish! Just like the liberty to name your child!

THE CORE OF NAMING YOUR SAMPLE…

It is the responsibility of MAN to name things on earth… You are already naming your world now.

It must be spoken out…. Your mouth is your life.

It must be specific. Clarity and specificity are vital in naming your sample.

It must be convincing to you… You must see yourself having and owning it… It must be at your developed Faith… At the level believable to you.

It must be SPOKEN OUT and BOLDLY DECLARED to become your MIRACLE SAMPLE. The power is in your speaking it forth. Man has been given the Will to Choose. What you choose is what is only permitted to happen to you. Hence, as you name your sample, it becomes it. Think about the names around you today.

SOME EXAMPLES IN THE BIBLE...

- Samson named his last attempt as ONE BLOW of VENGEANCE against the Philistines, and he killed more that day than all he ever did in his lifetime. (Judges 16:28, 30).

- David named his service of killing Goliath the Battle of the Lord, and GOD took over and used ordinary stone to kill a skilful warrior... (1 Samuel 17:37, 45-47).

- A widow of a prophet was asked by Elisha what she had, she named it, a jar of oil... and she became an oil merchant... (2 Kings 4:1-7).

- A small boy gave his lunch (five loaves of bread and two fish) that fed five thousand plus people with multiple loaves of Bread and Fish (John 6: 1-13).

Today, GOD is still expecting you to NAME your world, for it is what you call it that it becomes. You are already naming your world daily; however, GOD wants you to name your world creatively and consciously, creating miracles in view. It is a crucial element in creating miracles... Your specific, bold declaration of the desired name will birth the same in reality!

Your Notes. . .

PRACTISING - NAME YOUR SAMPLE...

Take your already identified sample and call it your desired miracle. Be specific. For example, if your sample is money, hold the money in your hand, or by faith, if the money is not in cash, and proclaim... 'This $100 is my healing from this illness'... Or, 'My interpreting in Church Service' is my Miracle Sample for my Marital Restoration... Or, This my 'Landed property' is my 'Business breakthrough,'... etc.

Practise and Name your Sample now...

CREATING YOUR MIRACLE...NOW! (3 OF 7)... CHANGE KINGDOM INTO CHRIST'S.

Do you know that two different kingdoms are operating right now in this world?... The Kingdom of CHRIST and the kingdom of Darkness?

Do you also know that this Earth was cursed because of the sins committed by Adam? Therefore, the world is functioning below its expectation and is prone to accidents, abnormalities, and attacks from the forces of darkness?

> *Do you know that two different kingdoms are operating right now in this world? … The Kingdom of CHRIST and the kingdom of darkness?*
>
> *Thus your MIRACLES are hidden for your good. However, it needs to be insured under the Kingdom of CHRIST...*

Thus your MIRACLES are hidden for your good. However, it needs to be insured under the Kingdom of GOD, which is CHRIST...

How much of the Kingdom of CHRIST do you know? Only in the Kingdom of Christ is the guarantee of safety, orderliness, assurance of the desired outcome, void of accidents, errors, and attacks from the forces of darkness.

WHY TRANSFER YOUR SAMPLE INTO THE KINGDOM OF CHRIST.

The Kingdom of this world is cursed and incapable of successfully delivering as expected of what you sow. It is unpredictable and can birth thorns, thistles, toil, labour, and perversion... It is only in the Kingdom of GOD that expected multiplications and reproduction are guaranteed...

Therefore, the need to transfer your SAMPLE, appropriately named into the Dominion of CHRIST, where it can birth the same. Dedicating your Sample unto GOD and BLESSING it in the NAME of JESUS CHRIST...

Our Lord JESUS CHRIST, when creating the miracle to feed five thousand plus people with only five loaves of bread and two fishes, requested that they bring the samples to Him. He took the samples, lifted His eyes to Heaven and BLESSED the sample pieces of bread and fish before Giving them back to his disciples for distribution. (Matthew 14:19).

That simple and singular act is He exchanging Kingdom for the His kingdom where multiplications can occur without interruptions or disturbances. This step was skilfully observed in many of our Lord JESUS CHRIST's miracles.

HOW TO TRANSFER YOUR SAMPLE INTO THE KINGDOM OF CHRIST...

I. START WITH SALVATION ...

It starts from you being translated into the Kingdom of GOD. When you receive CHRIST as your Lord and Saviour, you were delivered from the dominion of darkness and translated into the kingdom of CHRIST. (Colossian 1:13).

II. BELIEVE IN THE EXISTENCE OF THE KINGDOM OF CHRIST...

Our Lord JESUS CHRIST repeatedly confirmed that this earthly realm is not His kingdom. There is a kingdom of Light, different in operation from the kingdom at work on this earth. And we are expected to seek how this kingdom operates. (Matthew 6:33; John 18:36; Colossians 1: 13-14)

III. BELIEVE IN THE SUPERIORITY OF THE KINGDOM OF CHRIST...

The Kingdom of CHRIST is positioned far above all principalities and power, and might and dominion, and every name named, not only in this age but also in that which is to come. **Understanding this assures you that anything you transact in the kingdom of CHRIST is beyond the reach of the cursed earth and evil ones of the darkness...** (Ephesians 1: 19-23)

IV. BELIEVE IN YOUR JOINT HEIR WITH CHRIST...

When you receive JESUS CHRIST, you also partake of His divine nature and become a joint heir of all things with Him. Understanding this will boost your confidence in accessing your right to the kingdom of CHRIST. (Romans 8:17; Galatians 4:6-7; Ephesians 2:4-6).

V. UNDERSTANDS THAT THE KINGDOM OF CHRIST OPERATES ONLY BY FAITH.

For the just shall live by Faith. We are sons of God through faith in CHRIST JESUS. For it is of faith that it might be according to GRACE so that the promise might be sure to all the seed. . . (Hebrews 10:38; Galatians 3:26; Romans 4:16)

VI. TRANSFER YOUR MIRACLE SAMPLE INTO THE KINGDOM OF CHRIST...

BLESS your miracle sample in the Name of our Lord JESUS CHRIST, consecrate it and dedicate it to the Kingdom of CHRIST. This step is vital in your journey to create your desired miracle.

Once you proclaim the BLESSING of GOD upon it, it changes dominion from that of this cursed world and the influence and interference of the kingdom of darkness. Hence, it overcomes the world as it is now born of GOD. (Colossian 1:13; 1 John 5:4).

SOME MORE EXAMPLES IN THE BIBLE...

- When Potiphar handed over his house to Joseph, his home flourished because he unknowingly changed the kingdom to that of GOD. He acknowledged the Hand of GOD upon Joseph afterwards. (Genesis 39:2-4)

> *Remember that the supernatural is normal and natural in the Kingdom of GOD...*

- David turned his fight against Goliath unto the Lord. He said this battle is the Lord's. (1 Samuel 17: 47).

- Our Lord JESUS CHRIST took the bread and fish samples, lifted His eyes unto heaven and BLESSED them... (Matthew 14:19)

- At the Grave of Lazarus, our Lord JESUS CHRIST lifted His eyes and thanked GOD... (John 11:41).

REMEMBER THAT THE SUPERNATURAL IS NORMAL AND NATURAL IN THE KINGDOM OF GOD...

IF YOU DO NOT GET your desired RESULT... CHECK YOURSELF... SOMETHING may be WRONG WITH WHAT YOU ARE THINKING, SAYING AND DOING... Because this is a spiritual law that governs the Kingdom of CHRIST. It is operating regardless of you. Hence, it will work for you any time and every time. This step is critical in your journey to create your desired miracle.

Your Notes. . .

PRACTISING CHANGE KINGDOM INTO CHRIST…

Changing Kingdom into Christ's is a very, very simple step, yet significant. BLESS your miracle sample in the Name of our Lord JESUS CHRIST, consecrate it and dedicate it to the Kingdom of CHRIST.

Simply say… I BLESS you … my Healing, in the Name of JESUS CHRIST, or I BLESS you my marital restoration in the Name of JESUS CHRIST, or I BLESS you my Business breakthrough … Remember, you have named your sample; hence, you should call the name as such henceforth!

CREATING YOUR MIRACLE...NOW! (4 OF 7)... AGREE WITH GOD.

Do you know that FAITH is the only means of communication and transactions in the Kingdom of CHRIST?

Do you know that FAITH is NEUTRAL...; it tilts to the highest knowledge bidder?

> *Without faith... it is impossible to please GOD!*
>
> *FAITH is the only means of communication, and FAITH is the only means of transaction in the Kingdom of CHRIST.*

Do you also know that everyone is operating in FAITH right now?

The question is, what is your Faith focusing on right now?

This reason is why to access your hidden MIRACLES . . . Man must agree with GOD through Faith in His Word concerning the desired miracles...

Therefore, in creating your miracle now..., a critical step is to Agree with GOD!

WHY AGREE WITH GOD . . . ON YOUR MIRACLE?

WITHOUT FAITH... IT IS IMPOSSIBLE TO PLEASE GOD!

FAITH is the means of communication, and FAITH is the means of transaction in the Kingdom of CHRIST. In this world, English,

Spanish, Chinese, etc., are the major means of communication, while Pound Sterling, Dollar, Yen, Rand, Dirham, etc., are means of transaction. In the kingdom of GOD, only FAITH speaks! Hence, without Faith, it is impossible to please GOD (Hebrews 11:6). GOD is not a respecter of persons; HE is a respecter of Faith.

THE KINGDOM OF CHRIST OPERATES SOLELY BY FAITH.

First John 5:14-15 says this is our confidence, that when we ask anything according to His will, He hears us and is assured that we will have our petition. Your miracles are hidden for you in the kingdom of CHRIST; for you to access them, you must speak the language of GOD, FAITH...

YOUR MIRACLES MUST BE IN LINE WITH GOD'S WORD...

Whatever the miracle you intend to create, to be successful in this, it must be in line with the Word of GOD for your life now! What is the Word of GOD saying about your desired miracle? The good news is that your name is written in the Bible; your situation is well covered in the scriptures... and your expected desired miracle is hidden in the scriptures.

So, go and search them out.

 GOD PERFORMS ONLY HIS WORD...

GOD is committed to His Word and will keep it no matter what!

GOD watches out for His Word in any man or situation to perform it. Therefore, to get GOD to do anything for you, you must first get HIS word to agree with it.

HOW DO YOU AGREE WITH GOD … ON THAT MIRACLE?

I. SEARCH THE SCRIPTURES ON YOUR EXPECTED MIRACLE …

It is your responsibility to align with the Word of GOD. Use the mobile Bible gadgets today, type your current situation or your expected miracles, read all the scriptures that pop up on it and lay hold on two or three of them that resonate well with you.

II. MEDITATE ON THE WORD UNTIL YOU HIT THE POINT OF FAITH…

Spend time reading, studying and meditating on the selected word. 'WAIT' on these scriptures until you are fully persuaded that God is speaking to you directly through them. As you believe the word of God, you are agreeing with GOD. This process may not happen overnight. So, go to work on it.

Forever, the Word of God is settled. (Psalms 119:89). GOD declared boldly in Isaiah 55: 8-11 that none of His word will return to Him void.

'For as the rain comes down, and the snow from heaven, And do not return there, But water the earth, And make it bring forth and

168

bud, That it may give seed to the sower and bread to the eater, [11]
*So shall My word be that goes forth from My mouth; It shall not
return to Me void, But it shall accomplish what I please, And it shall
prosper in the thing for which I sent it.' (Isaiah 55: 10-11 NKJV)*

However, because we are used to parents lying, governments not
keeping their words, and friends and family members defrauding
one, many tend to carry this mindset into relating to GOD. You
must break through that and embrace the inerrancy of GOD's
word … (the inability of God's Word to fail).

Once fully persuaded by the Word of God for your miracle, make
such Word your final authority.

This statement, I mean, regardless of what you see, feel, or
circumstances surrounding your expected miracle, let the Word of
GOD be your final authority. Final stand, last stop, final decision,
final point!

Declare boldly and stick with the chosen Word of GOD on your
miracle. Stay put on it. Speak it, Chant it, Declare it and stick with
it no matter what.

Engage the Word until the Spirit of God speaks the Word into your
Spirit. Engage the Word until you receive your Evidence and Proof
of Faith… This way, you are agreeing with GOD on your desired
miracle, a critical step to creating the miracle.

CHECKING IF YOU ARE AGREEING WITH GOD ON YOUR DESIRED MIRACLE...

Can you say YES to the following questions?

1. Is this miracle the will of GOD for you?

2. Can GOD make this miracle happen?

3. Will GOD grant you this miracle?

4. Why will GOD grant you this miracle?

5. Do you deserve this miracle?

If you are unsure of a YES to one or more of the questions above, doubts are still lurking around; it is time to go back to the scriptures and 'wait' some more on them until you are fully persuaded. Then you are agreeing with GOD.

SOME MORE EXAMPLES IN THE BIBLE...

David exalted the GOD of Israel and turned the battle against Goliath unto the Lord. He proclaimed God's ability to deliver with few and with many. And GOD won for him. (1 Samuel 19: 45-47)

Hannah agreed with the Word of God through the prophet, Eli, and she went away happy and returned with her testimony, A son named Samuel. (1 Samuel 1:17-18).

The widow in 2 Kings 4:1-2 went to the Prophet of God, Elisha, for her miracle. She obeyed what the prophet told her to do.

The woman with the issue of blood in Mark 5:28 remarkably upheld a custom of the Jews —'The Priest Garments are as anointed and sacred as the priests' (Exodus 29:21; 35:19). Hence agreed that if she could touch our Lord, JESUS's garment, she would be made whole.

The Syrophoenician Woman in Mark 7:26-29 was convinced she had a right to healing, and her daughter was healed.

REMEMBER THAT THE SUPERNATURAL IS NORMAL AND NATURAL IN THE KINGDOM OF GOD...

IF YOU DO NOT GET your desired RESULT... CHECK YOURSELF... SOMETHING may be WRONG WITH WHAT YOU ARE THINKING, SAYING AND DOING... Because this is a spiritual law that governs the Kingdom of CHRIST. It is operating regardless of you. Hence, it will work for you any time and every time.

Your Notes. . .

PRACTISING - AGREEING WITH GOD...

This step is the longest in your journey of creating your miracle. This is because you cannot fake Agreeing with GOD. If you do not agree, it will show.

To practice this, engage the scriptures you are standing on and meditate until you hit the Point of Faith; this can be hastened by focusing on clearing your hearing channels off thoughts... Once your hearing channel is cleared of wondering and doubting thoughts, the Spirit of God will speak the word back to you... This is agreeing with GOD.

How are you going to practice this in your circumstances?

CREATING YOUR MIRACLE...NOW! (5 OF 7)... RELEASE YOUR SAMPLE

There must be that point of contact with the Kingdom of CHRIST.

> *There must be that point of contact with the Kingdom of CHRIST.*
>
> *This is when your sample leaves you to CHRIST...this is when the miracles are being contracted... The point when you receive your miracle...*

This point is when your sample leaves you to CHRIST...this is when the miracles are being contracted... The moment when you receive your miracle...

Once you release your sample, it is already too late for it not to happen...

When do you release your sample?

Where do you release your sample? How do you release your sample? Where is Christ's Point on earth? Who are Christ's Points on the earth? Let us take a deep dive into these...

RELEASE YOUR SAMPLE...

Releasing your Sample is the point of contact with the Anointing... A moment of contact with the Kingdom of CHRIST... The woman

173

with the issue of blood... in *Mark 5: 27-28, "When she heard about Jesus, she came behind him in the crowd and touched his garment. For she said, "if only I may touch His clothes, I shall be made well."*

If only I may but touch His garment... and she touched our LORD JESUS CHRIST's Garment. At the point of contact, she received her miracle...not before... not after...at that instant...

Today, our LORD JESUS CHRIST is not physically present on the earth now. He is not at any location today, hence the need to have a point of contact with His Anointing...

You have a sample, named it your miracle sample, BLESSED it and moved it into the Kingdom of CHRIST... You have also agreed with GOD on it, speaking the language of the kingdom... FAITH... Now... you have to release your sample...

When do you release your sample... Whereinto do you release your sample... And how do you release your sample...

WHEN DO YOU RELEASE YOUR SAMPLE...?

When the atmosphere has shifted ... into an atmosphere of the Kingdom of CHRIST... As you brood on the word of God concerning your miracle..., you get to a point when your heart synchronized with the word... when fully persuaded... it can be called ... the

174

boiling point... A point you fully agree with GOD that He can and will grant you your miracle based on His word.

Some characteristics of the right atmosphere to release your sample are - an unexplainable joy; - peace that passes all understanding ... - full persuasion... - the presence of the Anointing. When you see these things, it is time to release your sample...

This point of Releasing your Sample is your point of contact with the Anointing... it is your receiving point...not your believing point...

WHERE DO YOU RELEASE *YOUR SAMPLE INTO...?*

Where is the kingdom of CHRIST?

This point of Releasing your sample is your point of contact with the Anointing... it is your receiving point...not your believing point...

In the world today... Our Lord JESUS CHRIST is not physically present...; however, He is still present... He said He is the Head of the Church, and every member is part of His body... (Ephesians 1:22-23; 5:23; Colossians 1:18)

Hence, there are representatives of the Kingdom of CHRIST platforms in this world...They represent CHRIST and can serve as your point of contact to the Anointing. They are:

- The Churches... anywhere named with JESUS CHRIST... as Lord, carrying out services of the Kingdom.

- The Ministries... Ventures, Services, Teaching Ministry, Outreaches, etc. that focus on the Gospel and Christ's kingdom...

- The Ministers... They are the Apostles... the Prophets... the Evangelists... the Pastors... the Teachers... Anointed by GOD to function in the Body of CHRIST.

These places or people can be used as a point of contact to CHRIST's Anointing... These are the representatives of CHRIST on earth... Here, you can release your sample into the church, give that service, give that material item, or give that 'named money' to that minister, ministry or church where Christ's faith is expressed and practised...

POINT OF NOTE...

Releasing your Miracle Sample is not an offering; it is not a gift, contribution or donation... Always remember that as you yield to the SPIRIT of GOD, to lead you to the choice Kingdom of CHRIST platform to release your sample...

176

Also, very importantly, the different platforms carry different degrees of CHRIST... because FAITH and Kingdom principles are permitted in varying degrees in churches, ministries and among various ministers... Even in good lands, yield may still bring forth 30, 60 or 100 folds. (Mark 4: 20). Therefore, choose wisely.

Therefore, let the Holy Spirit lead you to platforms where FAITH and such principles of Christ's Kingdom are often preached and practised. Seek proof that your desired miracles are working in the lives of such a Minister, Ministry or the Church.

Remember ... this is your point of contact with the ANOINTING of CHRIST... Hence take it seriously... it is not an offering or support to any church, ministry, man or woman of GOD. It is releasing your miracle sample into CHRIST's Kingdom platform ... for reproduction...

HOW DO YOU RELEASE YOUR SAMPLE...?

DECLARE BOLDLY... that at the point of contact with this CHRIST Kingdom's platform ... your miracle will be born...

BE VERY SPECIFIC... as I take this action, service... in this platform..., my miracle is born...

TAKE ACTION... and release your miracle sample into the kingdom of CHRIST's platform you are led into... if your sample is a service...take action and render that service; If it is a material item or money, release it into the declared church, ministry or minister.

DEPART WITH THANKSGIVING AND REJOICING... This step is very important. Your joy and change of countenance indicate your receiving... This stage is a point of contact for receiving, not when to start believing...

REFERENCE THIS TIME... as your point of contact for your miracle... Always remember and reference that this is when your miracle is born... Anytime the thought of your miracle comes to mind, reference when it was received and thank GOD for your miracle... This attitude is a show of Faith...

Believing that God can never lie...

SOME MORE EXAMPLES IN THE BIBLE...

The widow in 2 Kings 4:1 cried out to Elisha the prophet, the representative of GOD in their days.

David went to King Saul... who prayed for him and bid him well in the battle against Goliath... (1 Samuel 17:37)

The woman with the issue of blood went out, looked for our Lord JESUS CHRIST, pressed to his location amid the crowd... and touched His garment. (Mark 5:27-28)

The prodigal son left his place of suffering to go to his father...and got to his father... (Luke 15:18-20).

Samson asked a small boy to lead him to the strong pillar of the building that the philistines gather to mock him... and he pushed as he had prayed. (Judges 16: 26-30).

The five loaves of bread and two fishes were brought to our Lord JESUS CHRIST... (Matthew 14: 16-19).

There are two more steps to go... Now that you have your miracle, which most likely is hidden in the spiritual... how do you translate it into physical manifestations... and partake of it physically in actual times? Seeing the miracles right before your face...

Your Notes. . .

PRACTISING - RELEASE YOUR SAMPLE...

Take action: Release your miracle sample into the kingdom of CHRIST's platform you are led into... if your sample is a service...take action and render that service; If it is a material item or money, release it into the declared church, ministry or man or woman of GOD.

To practice this... Speak forth: **I take this Church, this Ministry, or this Man or Woman of GOD, as my point of contact to the Anointing of CHRIST. Therefore, as I give this material thing ..., as I give this money ..., or as I release my sample to this point of contact, I will receive my miracle in the Name of JESUS CHRIST, Amen...** Then take action and release it...

You can practice this now.

CREATING YOUR MIRACLE... NOW! (6 OF 7)... HARVEST YOUR MIRACLE PASSCODE...

The whole 'Create your miracle... Now!' series can be grouped into two categories...

- Create your miracle...

- Harvest your miracle...

Up until now, we have been looking at how to create your miracle:

What do you have...? Name your Sample... Change Kingdom into CHRIST's... Agree with GOD... and Release your Miracle Sample...

Now that your miracle is created..., it is imperative to move into HOW to harvest your miracle.

> *Your Miracle is hidden... for your good, so the evil eyes of darkness and corruptions in the world do not corrupt it.*
> *It is why your miracle is coded.*

Your Miracle is hidden... for your good, so the evil eyes of darkness and corruptions in the world do not corrupt it. It is why your miracle is coded. Even as you have received your miracle, it is hidden, not shown to everybody to see... Hence you need a 'miracle passcode' to access your miracle. Why do you need a miracle passcode?

WHY MIRACLE PASSCODE?

GOD is not in complete control of this world... He could, however, chooses not to because He seeded the earth to man!

The Bible says in *Psalms 115:16, '... the earth GOD has given to the children of men'*. Therefore, for GOD to operate on this earth, He has to work indirectly through a man.

Most of the miracles needed by men are earthly bound. They are governed and influenced by the different laws operational in this world, such as Government laws, economic laws, legal laws, natural laws, common sense, scientific laws, etc. Therefore, in dispensing your miracle, GOD birth SUPERNATURAL in the most NATURAL WAY... Hence a need for a passcode.

I. THE ENEMY IS IN CONTROL OF THIS WORLD

Satan and his cohort hijacked the ruler-ship of the earth and this world from the first man, Adam, when they committed treason and lost their place of dominion with GOD.

2 Corinthians 4:3-4, Ephesians 2:2-3, and 2 Thessalonians 2:7 all confirm the force of darkness as the prince of the air, ruling over the children of disobedience.

This force of darkness is responsible for the evil calamities that befall the world and man. Therefore, if your miracle is not coded from them, they can still corrupt and steal it from you. (John 10:10). Hence the need for a miracle passcode.

II. TO SHOWCASE THE MULTI-FACETED WISDOM OF GOD...

As you manifest your miracle, you are showing forth the unique wisdom of GOD in this world. Showcasing the unending ways of GOD, the unfathomable wisdom of GOD. For His ways past finding out. (Romans 11:33).

'Oh, the depth of the riches both of the wisdom and knowledge of God! How unsearchable are His judgements and His ways past finding out!' (Romans 11:33 NKJV)

III. TO DISPLAY THE SUPREMACY OF GOD AND HIS CHRIST.

The Bible in Hebrews 1:1-4 describes our Lord JESUS CHRIST as the Heir of all things, through whom all things were created, the brightness of God's Glory, the express image of GOD... upholding all things by the Word of his Power.

Even though GOD has conceded the earth to man... HE still has supremacy power over it whenever He chooses to. **When you manifest your miracle, you display the supremacy of GOD and HIS CHRIST over the earth, darkness and this world.**

IV. TO BUILD BELIEVER'S DEPENDENCY ON GOD'S WORD...

As you partake in the Divine nature of GOD through the manifestation of signs and wonders in miracles, your faith and dependence on GOD's Word are built. You become bold to face future challenges... **As a matter of fact, once you win twice or more, the enemy tries to avoid you like the plague!**

WHO REVEALS MIRACLE PASSCODES?

THE HOLY SPIRIT...

The Holy Spirit is the one that reveals your miracle passcode...

The Holy Spirit also unravel your miracle passcode... its detailing.

The Holy Spirit also empowers you to apply the revealed miracle passcode...

1 Corinthians 2:9-10 says that '... Eye has not seen, nor ear heard, nor have entered into the heart of man, the things which God has prepared for those who love HIM..,

 But God has revealed them to us through HIS SPIRIT. For the Spirit searches all things, yes, the deep things of God. (NKJV).

Now that you understand the principle behind the miracle passcode, how will one lay hold on the miracle passcode? How does one harvest the miracle passcode in reality?

HOW TO HARVEST YOUR MIRACLE PASSCODE...

I. RECOGNIZE & ACKNOWLEDGE THE HARVEST STAGE.

Be confident and excited about this stage. Be full of thanksgiving. This session is not praying or believing time; it is harvesting time. As you recognize this, you become aware and expectant of your passcode, way out, and open-door to your miracle.

Your miracle passcode will be released at the Boiling Point of your prayer. This point is when the Holy Spirit has taken over the Word and speaking it forth through you... In that atmosphere of the Point of Faith... The Holy Spirit will also give you an instruction, actionable plan, and command that you need to take...

Remember, God has His part, and you have your part to birth your desired miracle... GOD does the supernatural; Man does the natural, to give birth to the supernatural naturally.

II. YOUR PASSCODE WILL BE CONCEALED...

It is essential to understand the nature of miracle passcodes... They are concealed, hidden, may not be regular, may seem so 'senseless' to human intelligence, may look so simple and easy. However, it will always be something within your reach and do-a-able for you!

This concealing is intentional, so the evil eyes may not easily code what you are up to until its full manifestation. Such was boy David, who used ordinary stone to kill a seasoned, giant, terrifying warrior named Goliath. (1 Samuel 17:49).

Goliath saw a small boy with a stick, and he became unguarded and planned to teach him a lesson; however, without his shield and at the least time expected, David brought out STONE from his cow boy's sheath... The stone was concealed... before Goliath could reach for his shield; he was already on the floor. GOD was with David and the rock, primarily... Goliath only saw the stick in David's hand... The stone was hidden from the enemy's prying eyes... Alleluia.

III. BELIEVE YOUR MIRACLE PASSCODE...

The responsibility is on you to believe your miracle passcode, thus why you are being shown today. Now that you have created your miracle, you are in the harvest stage; hence, a need to pay attention to the leading of the Holy Spirit. New directions, ideas, suggestions, visions, revelations and insights will be revealed to you. Believing this revelation is key to harvesting your miracles!

Though they may seem straightforward and easy compared to the mountainous problem facing you, BELIEVE them... and pay attention to obey them, for they are your miracle passcodes to the manifestation of your miracle.

Believe them, trust them. An example was Simon Peter, who was instructed to cast his NETS for a drought after he borrowed our Lord JESUS CHRIST his boat for preaching. He doubted this passcode; however, he only tried one NET... and was surprised at the many fishes caught at the oddest fishing time possible. He did not expect such a supernatural harvest! (Luke 5:4-8).

IV. KEEP YOUR PASSCODE SAFE...

It is important to note that your miracle passcode is kept secret as much as possible. They are access to your miracle, do not show it forth to the world yet, less it is stolen and corrupted.

The widow that went to Elisha for a miracle was told to close her doors behind her while discharging her miracle passcode. (2 Kings 4:4). Our Lord JESUS CHRIST often closes the door and sends out a doubting multitude in the face of miracles.

SOME MORE EXAMPLES IN THE BIBLE...

- Jacob saw stripes animals as his miracle passcode, and he mimicked it and prospered thereby... (Genesis 30:37-39).

- Prophet Elisha told the widow to shut her door behind her as she discharged her miracle passcode... (2 Kings 4:4)

- Elisha told Naaman to go and wash in river Jordan seven times; he went and was healed of leprosy. (2 Kings 5:9-10, 14).

- David hid his stones in his bag while holding a stick when approaching Goliath to kill him... (1 Samuel 17:49).

- Our Lord JESUS CHRIST told Peter to get the very first fish and found a Gold coin in its mouth to pay for their tax... (Matt. 17:27).

- Our Lord JESUS CHRIST distributed the BLESSED few loaves of bread and fishes with the 12 disciples first, not the crowd... And as it went round the disciples, they did same to the multitude of over five thousand… and return with leftovers! (John 6: 11)

Many other examples of engaging miracle passcodes for miracles in the Bible exist. As you pay attention to the leading of the Holy Ghost at the Point of Faith in your prayers, miracle passcodes will be released to you. Believe them, even if they sound or look simple and unintelligent, for God specializes in using the foolish things of the world to confound the wise, thus, showcasing His supremacy over the earth and universe.

Pause, Ponder, and Think about this today…

Your Notes. . .

PRACTISING - HARVEST YOUR MIRACLE PASSCODE…

At the Boiling Point of your Prayer… What is the Holy Spirit telling you to do…? These instructions may be simple, easy to do, unbelievably simple… like 'buy lunch for your boss'… It could be to stay at home and worship today… It could be to start a business idea that looks ridiculous… It could be to take a leave for a trip… Whatever it is, will be a customised passcode that you can do… without much effort… so you can participate in the miraculous in your life.

Have you started receiving your Miracle Passcodes? … What are they? Write them out here…

CREATE YOUR MIRACLE ... NOW! (7 OF 7)... HARVEST YOUR MIRACLE...

Finally, How do you harvest your miracle?

Do you know that after you have created your miracle... It is vital to understand HOW to harvest it?

How do you harvest your miracle? This step is taking the corresponding action based on your miracle passcode...

Act on the plan you received... As soon as possible.

This stage is where works come into play... As a believer... There is what you have to do... to harvest your miracle...

> *How do you harvest your miracle? It is taking the corresponding action based on your miracle passcode...*

The difference between believers' works and others are...

You work from answers... You are working by Divine instructions... You are working based on the revealed miracle passcode... You are expectant of an Overflow...

You are working beyond Labour and Toil... It is a targeted work!

In the world system, there is labour and toil. Adam was cursed and reduced to labour and toiling; this curse is still in operation today.

190

Trial and error, Struggle, struggle and struggle... Working for survival... The rat race... are the order of the day in the world.

However, in the Kingdom of CHRIST... Like in the beginning, you work from the place of Rest with guaranteed success!

In 'CREATE YOUR MIRACLE ...NOW'...

You are not just working; you are taking action based on your miracle passcode. (Step 6). Apostle Peter, a fisherman, in Matthew 17:27, was instructed by Our Lord Jesus Christ to cash the very first fish and therein lay a Gold coin in its mouth for their tax payment. He was only to cash one fish!

When you work on your miracle passcode, you become the Hands of GOD for signs and wonders...

Through you... GOD's multi-faceted wisdom and supremacy are displayed.

He did not need to catch 100 fish, clean them up, take them to the market, and sell them to get enough money to pay their tax. He took a step on his miracle passcode and got an overflow. The very first fish was enough!

When you work based on your miracle passcode, you work less... sweat less... no labour... no toiling... In addition, as you work... You

191

hit a breakthrough... An Overflow... Since the work is simply a channel for the manifestation of the miraculous. I pray that such become your regular daily experiences in prayers in the Name of Yeshua Hamashiach (Jesus Christ), Amen.

WHY WORK TO HARVEST YOUR MIRACLE?

I. YOU WORK BECAUSE GOD DO NOT LIKE LAZY HANDS...

The second book of Thessalonians 3:10 stated, ' *If anyone will not work, neither shall he eat.' James 2:17 stated clearly that '... Faith by itself, if it does not have works, is dead'. It is important to note that* the work must be born from Faith, not working to impress or bribe God or validate your faith! It is working at the Point of Faith!

II. SO YOUR MIRACLE LOOKS LEGITIMATE HERE ON EARTH...

You work, so your miracle looks legitimate here on earth. GOD will birth the supernatural in the most natural way. GOD is not an author of confusion. Hence, an element of work is needed for your miracle's manifestation, no matter how small the work is.

III. YOU WORK ONLY ON YOUR MIRACLE PASSCODE...

You are to work only based on the miracle passcode received at the point of faith in prayers. When you work ONLY based on your miracle passcode, you access the full barking of heaven with all the divine resources available to you... since you are simply taking action on Divine instructions...

IV. YOU BECOME THE HAND OF GOD FOR SIGNS AND WONDER...

When you work on your miracle passcode, you become the Hand of GOD for signs and wonders... Through you... GOD's multi-faceted wisdom and supremacy are displayed.

HOW DO YOU HARVEST YOUR MIRACLE...?

- Harvest your Miracle Passcode...

- Believe your Miracle Passcode...

- Take the Corresponding Action based on the passcode...

- Take steps in line with the received plans. Follow your instinct on steps to take...

They may be outrageous... Follow them. Here, you will need more of a COURAGE to STEP OUT...

Make steps with speed... Swiftly... Some actions may require some preparation..., and others may be swift. However, they will be something within your reach... And as you take steps, you will experience your miracle...

EXPECT AN OVERFLOW...

GOD will always bring you into an overflow... More than enough... The overflow is the substance of the Sabbath... It is the way of

GOD...Always! God demonstrated this with the Israelites through the Sabbath... let's quickly see it in operation...

Genesis 2:1-3 declared that the creation of the heavens, earth, and all the hosts was complete, and God rested on the seventh day and BLESSED it as a Holy day.

The Prophet, Moses, being led by GOD, taught and instructed the Israelites to observe the Sabbath.., no labour, shown by a double portion of 'Manna' on the 6th day to cater for the 7th day. (Exodus 16:23). Why no work... Because there is an overflow... A double portion...enough to cater for the Sabbath.

Furthermore, there is the Sabbath Year, a whole year of no labour and toil. This rest was possible because GOD BLESSED them so much in the 6th year, enough to last for three years. (Leviticus 25:4, 20-21).

> *What guarantees a Sabbath rest is the prior laid down provision!*

There was also the Year of Jubilee... The 50th year, No labour and toil that year too. However, since the 49th year was also a Sabbath, the Israelites could not labour and toil for two whole years... When they asked how they would survive these three years before the harvest of the 51st year, the Lord said, HE will

194

BLESS the 48th year harvest so much that it will outlast the three years... Alleluia! Amen. (Leviticus 25:11, 13)

What guarantees a Sabbath rest is the prior laid down provision! However, these are a type and a shadow of things to come. Our Lord JESUS CHRIST said HE is the LORD of the Sabbath. (Mark 2:28). Colossians 2:16-17 made it clear that the emphasis should not be on the ceremony of the Sabbath, for the SUBSTANCE OF SABBATH IS CHRIST! Hebrews 4:9 made it clear that 'FOR THERE IS YET REMAIN... A REST TO THE PEOPLE OF GOD...

When you bought into CHRIST, you bought into the Sabbath Rest, where you cease from labour and toiling as everything is ready for you. CHRIST is the substance of the Sabbath.

[9] 'There remains therefore a rest for the people of God. [10] For he who has entered His rest has himself also ceased from his works as God did from His.' (Hebrews 4:9-10 NKJV)

My dear friend, what will you rather do with this information? This Overflow... (Sabbath Rest) was greatly inspired by the messages of Br. [5]Gary Keesee on 'Sabbath Rest'... Please search and listen to them; he also has a book on this... Please avail yourself of his resources...He is a BLESSING!

You can cease from that labour, struggle, toiling, and oppression. Sickness, bondage and affliction, and begin to create your desired miracles from today.

If you taste the GOODNESS of GOD once or twice, you will never remain the same. Join the saints that are living in the Sabbath Rest of GOD today. Create your miracle... NOW!

RETURN TO GIVE GOD ... ALL THE PRAISE.

As you experience the Goodness of GOD in your life, it is essential that you return to give GOD all the praise. For as you acknowledge and return to give GOD thanks, HE sees to it that you attract more of HIS GOODNESS. (Mark 4:25).

SOME MORE EXAMPLES IN THE BIBLE...

Jacob saw spotted animals as his passcode, and he created them in actual times and prospered therein. (Genesis 30:37-43).

A widow instructed by Elisha, borrowed vessels, poured oil from her tiny jar by faith, sold them and prospered... (2 Kings 4:1-7)

David went to the brook and got him smooth stones that he used to kill a seasoned warrior, Goliath... (1 Samuel 17:40)

Samson pushed on the pillar of the Philistines' location... by faith, and he killed more people that day in his life... (Judges 16:30).

Peter went to the pool with a hook to catch the first fish and got a Gold coin in its mouth for their tax payment... (Matthew 17:27)

The woman with the issue of blood despised her weakness..., pressed in the crowd and touched the hem of the garment of our Lord JESUS CHRIST and was made whole... (Mark 5: 27-30).

The prodigal son... left the place of his suffering and went to his father... he was received into Blessing! (Luke 15:20).

You, too, can take action and reap a miracle... Now.

Remember that the supernatural is normal and natural in the Kingdom of GOD... if you get no result... Check yourself... Something may be wrong with what you are thinking, saying and doing... The word always works...once you follow the steps...

We pray that you are now better informed on how to create and harvest your desired miracles in the Name of YESHUA HAMASHIACH (JESUS CHRIST), Amen.

I can't wait to hear how you create miracles using this principle... Please remember to send your testimonies to us via our E mail: info@air.church

We believe that they will come through for you... in the Name of Yeshua Hamashiach (Jesus Christ), Amen. Shalom.

Your Notes. . .

PRACTISING - HARVEST YOUR MIRACLE...

Harvesting your Miracle is the time for action. You are taking steps in line with your miracle passcode... What is your miracle passcode...? Take the step now... Do not broadcast yet... Just take the steps... and hit the overflow.

Write out your Miracle passcode and take actions only based on them... Now!

Your Notes . . .

What miracle will you be creating this season?

Write it down as a reference... For it shall become a reality in the Name of YESHUA HAMASHIACH (JESUS CHRIST), Amen.

THE

FULLNESS

IN

CHRIST . . . .

Prayer Dynamics ...

THE FULLNESS IN CHRIST ···

THE FULLNESS OF CHRIST...

"The earth is the LORD's, and all its fullness, The world and those who dwell therein. For He has founded it upon the seas, And established it upon the waters." (Psalms 24:1-2 NKJV)

"And of His fullness we have all received, and grace for grace." (John 1:16 NKJV)

"And He put all things under His feet, and gave Him to be head over all things to the church, which is His body, the fullness of Him who fills all in all." (Ephesians 1:22-23 NKJV)

"For by Him all things were created that are in heaven and that are on earth, visible and invisible, whether thrones or dominions

or principalities or powers. All things were created through Him and for Him." (Colossians 1:16 NKJV)

"For it pleased the Father that in Him all the fullness should dwell," (Colossians 1:19 NKJV)

"For in Him dwells all the fullness of the Godhead bodily;" (Colossians 2:9 NKJV)

It pleased the Father that in our Lord JESUS CHRIST, all the Fullness should dwell!

'And you are complete in Him, who is the head of all principality and power.' (Colossians 2:10 NKJV)

'God, who at various times and in various ways spoke in time past to the fathers by the prophets, [2]has in these last days spoken to us by His Son, whom He has appointed heir of all things, through whom also He made the worlds;

[3]who being the brightness of His glory and the express image of His person, and upholding all things by the word of His power, when He had by Himself purged our sins, sat down at the right hand of the Majesty on high, [4]having become so much better than the angels, as He has by inheritance obtained a more excellent name than they.' (Hebrews 1:1-4 NKJV).

The Fullness of CHRIST... ALLELUIA!

WHAT IS THE FULLNESS IN CHRIST...

Some time ago, the Spirit of the Lord drew my attention to this powerful and all-fulfilling verse...

"For it pleased the Father that in Him all the fullness should dwell," *(Colossians 1:19 NKJV)*

It pleased the Father that in our Lord JESUS CHRIST, all the Fullness should dwell. This scripture is not a promise; it is affirming an already settled deal. So much it pleased the Father that all Fullness, without exception, dwell in CHRIST... Alleluia!

ALL THE FULLNESS... ALL OF IT... The fullness of the earth... The fullness of power... The fullness of favour... The fullness of Glory... The fullness of Peace... The fullness of Love... The fullness of Joy... The fullness of Righteousness... The fullness of Holiness... The fullness of Well-Being... The fullness of Wealth... The fullness of Discoveries... The fullness of Innovations... The fullness of Science, The fullness of Entertainment, The fullness of Health, The fullness of Medicine, The fullness of Agriculture, The fullness of Engineering, The fullness of Petroleum, The fullness of Politics, The fullness of Education, The fullness of Internet, The fullness of Transportation, The fullness of Fashion, The fullness of Pleasure,... The fullness of all...

ALL IN ALL... *"For it pleased the Father that in Him all the fullness should dwell,"* (Colossians 1:19 NKJV)

If all the Fullness is in CHRIST..., then every other thing, person or beings (including the Light angels, and the fallen angels --devil and demons), are having only 'A PART' of whatever they have.

The first Corinthians 13:9 says we know in parts... and we prophesy in parts... *"For we know in part and we prophesy in part."* *(I Corinthians 13:9 NKJV)*

Anyone with seemingly great gifts, endowments, skills, abilities, insights, breakthroughs ... Are given only in part!

For only in CHRIST JESUS, all the Fullness is.

If all the Fullness is in CHRIST..., then every other thing, person, or being are having only 'A PART' of whatever they have.

Colossians 1:16 further says that all things consist through CHRIST, and for CHRIST ... All things consist.

"For by Him all things were created that are in heaven and that are on earth, visible and invisible, whether thrones or dominions or principalities or powers. All things were created through Him and for Him." (Colossians 1:16 NKJV)

When are we going to believe this Truth? When is the Church going to embrace this Truth?

When will we stop pursuing Parts... and focus on the Source of all things? - CHRIST.

*James 1:17 says, "Every good gift and every perfect gift is from above, and comes down from the Father of lights, with whom there is no variation or shadow of turning." (*NKJV)

If all fullness is in CHRIST... It then means, in CHRIST and through CHRIST, the Church can access deeper Insights, Innovations, Gifting, Abilities, Favour, Wealth, Righteousness beyond this age, Holiness, Grace, Outstanding Miracles, Deliverance and Enablements...

SELAH... Pause, Ponder and Think about these things...

Do not quit too soon, do not give up so soon,

Fight for Your Salvation,

Fight for Your Righteousness...

Fight for Your Holiness...

Fight for Your Peace...

Fight for Your Marriage...

Fight for your Spouse ...

Fight for Your Family...

Fight for Your Children...

Fight for Your Long Life...

Fight for Your Sound Health...

Fight for your Ministry …

Fight for Your Prosperity...

Fight for Your Breakthrough...

Fight for Your Dominion...

Fight for Your Deliverance...

Fight The Good Fight Of Faith...

'It pleased the Father that in CHRIST JESUS, all the Fullness should dwell'...

Whatever your opponent is facing you with... is just a part... The Fullness is in CHRIST JESUS...

Whatever your opponent is facing you with... is just a part... The Fullness is in CHRIST JESUS...

The Good Part, The Free Part, The Love Part, The Help Part, The Deliverance Part, The Dominion Part, The Authority Part, The Missing Part... is in CHRIST JESUS!

And of His Fullness, we can receive the Qualifying Grace for the Reigning Grace!

"And of His fullness we have all received, <u>and grace for grace</u>." (John 1:16 NKJV)

The best is in CHRIST!

> *It is all about how much of CHRIST you carry…*
>
> *How much of CHRIST you can align with will make the difference in your life.*

In addition, CHRIST is waiting that through you and me (His Church)... His fullness might fill all in all... (Ephesians 1:23)

What will you rather do with this information, my dear friend?

Do not allow circumstances, situations, peer pressures, family, friends or the forces of darkness directly influence you to give in too soon … The Fullness of all is in CHRIST!

My father in the Lord, Br Kenneth E. Hagin, said in one of His messages… *'When you decide to wait forever until GOD's Word come to pass in your life… Then it won't take long!'.*

Do not give in too soon. There is no such thing as IT IS IMPOSSIBLE... NOT IN CHRIST!

WHY THE FULLNESS OF CHRIST...

In the MERCIES of GOD, I am sharing this with you today... It is all about CHRIST... It is all about how much of CHRIST you carry. How much of CHRIST you can align with will make the difference in your life. That will be your 'Game-Changer' in life!

In his teachings titled 'Intimacy with GOD', my father in the Lord, Br [6]Benny Hinn, delved extensively into the topic of 'Waiting in the Presence of GOD,' and so are other messages such as 'Practicing the Presence of GOD'... What a BLESSING to the Church...

When your alignment with CHRIST is sorted, Satan and all the forces of darkness become irrelevant... The PRESENCE OF CHRIST fights for you.

Please do avail yourself of these messages on YouTube or His website. The MERCY of GOD prevailed for Him that He was granted this rare privilege to access Intimacy with GOD.

His messages BLESS me immensely, thank you, and GOD BLESS you, Sir. Amen.

It is all about JESUS CHRIST...

How intimate you are with HIM will determine how much you will reign on this earth... and beyond, in Glory! When your alignment with CHRIST is sorted, Satan and all the forces of darkness become irrelevant... The PRESENCE OF CHRIST fights for you.

---

[6] Br Benny Hinn. www.bennyhinn.org

For in the presence of GOD, the evil forces cannot prey on Her; they do not even know her existence nor her mode of operation. The Presence o God is all of God! Alleluia.

'There is a path which no fowl knoweth, and which the vulture's eye hath not seen. The lion's whelps have not trodden it, nor the fierce lion passed by it.' (Job 28:7-8 KJV).

Witches and wizards, principalities, and Satan himself do not know nor has passed by her nor comprehend the Presence of GOD!

In the FULLNESS of CHRIST, the enemy can never see you nor be able to attack you. It is the Secret Place of the Most High.

'He who dwells in the secret place of the Most High Shall abide under the shadow of the Almighty.' (Psalms 91:1 NKJV).

Only in the Fullness of CHRIST is safety guaranteed.

> **When your alignment with CHRIST is sorted, Satan and all the forces of darkness become irrelevant…**

Only in the Fullness of CHRIST you will discover the real you and your full potential. *'For it pleased the Father, that in CHRIST JESUS, all Fullness should dwell'.(Colossians 1:19)*

When Simon discovered our Lord Jesus as 'CHRIST, the Son of the living GOD', he earned himself an identity he never knew he had… Peter! A rock… up until then, he saw himself as a weak man, son of Jonah; however, upon discovering who CHRIST is, He found himself as Peter, A Rock.

15 'He said to them, 'But who do you say that I am?' 16 Simon Peter answered and said, 'You are the Christ, the Son of the living God'. 17 Jesus answered and said to him, 'Blessed are you, Simon, Bar-Jonah, for flesh and blood has not revealed this to you, but My Father who is in heaven. 18 And I also say to you that you are Peter, and on this rock, I will build My church, and the gates of Hades shall not prevail against it.'' (Matthew 16:15-18 NKJV).

Today, if CHRIST asks you the same question… 'Who do you say CHRIST is?... what will be your answer?

Engaging the Fullness of CHRIST will never be a gift… It will never be something that just happened to you. It will only be what you consciously desire, long for, and pursue fully… It can only be born of your genuine love for God and His CHRIST!.

One day, the Spirit of GOD told me… ***'My love is not for sale'…***

In other words, I will not force Myself on anyone… My Spirit will not strive with men forever…

'And the Lord said, My Spirit shall not always strive with man, for that he also is flesh: yet his days shall be an hundred and twenty years.' (Genesis 6:3 NKJV)

If you do not reach out to seek the Presence of CHRIST, It will not happen to you automatically…

Pause, Ponder and Think about that!

However, through the Blood of JESUS CHRIST, everyone on this earth can partake and have access to the Secret Place of the Most High... The FULLNESS of CHRIST!

ENGAGING THE FULLNESS OF CHRIST AS A WEAPON...

You can use CHRIST's Fullness as a weapon by creating the Presence of CHRIST around you. When you manifest His Presence around you, He brings forth His Fullness and fixes your maimed, short, lacking, not enough, polluted or dead parts of your life.

Because it pleases the Father that in CHRIST all fullness should be. No matter what you need or want, the fullness is in CHRIST... No matter what has spoilt, destroyed or maimed in and around you... The Fullness of CHRIST can replace, repair and replenish...

When you consciously create the Presence of GOD around you... CHRIST's FULLNESS shows forth and fixes things for you. CHRIST Presence is also a terror to the forces of darkness, including your oppressors!

How then do you create this Presence of CHRIST?...

The Church has seen many that use these three major elements to create the Presence of GOD around them... Worship, The Word and Prayers. We all do them; why don't we all have the Presence of CHRIST enough to birth HIS FULLNESS for our advantage?

These elements are not new to the church. We worship GOD, read the scriptures, and pray in the Spirit. However, the gap preventing many from accessing Christ's Fulness through them is the amount of TIME SPENT IN WAITING...

The duration is where the secret lies... For the Presence of GOD will not just come because you command it. It will not happen because you are a pastor or a 'financier of the Gospel'... It will not arrive because the pastor loves you... The Presence of GOD will only manifest if believers spend enough time WAITING ON GOD...

> *The secret to the Presence of CHRIST's FULLNESS is in WAITING... DWELLING... KNOCKING... Spending time long enough until HE shows forth!*

Isaiah 30:15 says, *'For thus says the Lord God, the Holy One of Isreal: 'In returning and rest you shall be saved; In quietness and confidence shall be your strength.'' (NKJV).*

Psalms 91:1 says, *'He who dwells in the secret place of the Most High Shall abide under the shadow of the Almighty.'*

'But those who wait on the Lord Shall renew their strength, They shall mount up with wings like eagles, They shall run and not be weary, They shall walk and not faint. (Isaiah 40:31 NKJV)

[7]*'Ask, and it will be given you, seek, and you will find, knock, and it will be opened to you.* [8]*For everyone who asks receives, and he who seeks finds, and to him who knocks it will be opened.' (Matthew 7:7-8 NKJV).*

The secret to the Presence of CHRIST's FULLNESS is in WAITING... DWELLING... KNOCKING... Spending time long enough until HE shows forth!

When you spend time alone with GOD, you are blocking the enemy, self, thoughts, and all distractions out of your soul... Only then can CHRIST show forth... Only those who DWELL, WAIT, KNOCK... and ABIDE... long enough will encounter HIS FULLNESS.

Brother [7]Kenneth E. Hagin of Blessed memory spent time waiting on Ephesians chapters 1 and 3 for many months, and He encountered the Fullness of CHRIST. His ministry changed for the better; he gained deep insights into revelations that are a Blessing to the Church today.

> *The secret to the Presence of CHRIST's FULLNESS is in WAITING... DWELLING... KNOCKING... Spending time long enough until HE shows forth!*

Brother Benny Hinn used Worship to wait on GOD, and he encountered an intimacy with GOD. What a BLESSING he is to the church. Worship and Praise, Waiting on the Word of God, and Praying especially in the Spirit can be great tools in creating the Presence of CHRIST. Furthermore, it is imperative to understand the purpose of waiting to promote engagement. Let us take a quick and closer look at it now.

---

[7] Kenneth Hagin Ministries www.rhema.org

WHY WAIT ON GOD?...

You wait primarily to silence your soul before the Lord. A man's soul cannot worship GOD, yet man is a Spirit, has a Soul, and lives in a Body.

Your Soul is the seat of your Will, Mind (Intellect), and Emotion. Your Soul is what you use to engage the mortal world. Your Soul is where you store your experiences, memories, education, skills, characters, and intellect. Your Soul is accessible to the angelic realm and hence can be corrupted by the demons. The forces of darkness engage the mind of men to distract them from GOD and blindfold them from accessing the Glory of CHRIST.

'But even if our Gospel is veiled, it is veiled to those who are perishing, <u>whose minds the god of this age has blinded</u>, who do not believe, lest the light of the gospel of the glory of Christ, who is the image of God, should shine on them.' (2 Corinthians 4:3-4 NKJV).

³'For though we walk in the flesh, we do not war after the flesh. ⁴(For the weapons of our warfare are not carnal but mighty through God to the pulling down strongholds;) ⁵<u>casting down imaginations, and every high thing that exalteth itself against the knowledge of God, and bringing into captivity every thought to the obedience of Christ</u>; ⁶And having in a readiness to avenge all disobedience when your obedience is fulfilled.' (2 Corinthians 10:3-6 KJV).

The Mind of man is the primary barrier to entering the Presence of GOD. Many people Worship, study the scriptures and Pray in the Spirit; however, because their minds are not in it, they cannot prevail in prayers! Thus the reason why we wait on God!

When you WAIT on GOD, you silence the mind and shut out the thoughts, imaginations, and distractions, hence allowing the light of the Gospel of the Glory of CHRIST, who is the image of GOD, to shine on you.

You can use Worship and Praise and just stay on it... focusing on CHRIST in the songs until every thought and imagination submits and Christ reigns in you.

You can also use Waiting on the Word, not just reading the scriptures; waiting, meditating, and staying put until your attention is focused on the Word while insights and divine revelations pop out from the scriptures.

One day, the Spirit of GOD told me... 'The Word of God is not just the Bible; the Word of GOD is hidden inside the Bible; you need to dig deep to encounter the Word of Life.'

As you wait on the Word, insisting your thoughts and mind submit to what you are reading, silencing them and focusing on the scriptures, you will encounter CHRIST from them.

You can also use Praying in the Spirit... Just continue to Mingle with the Holy Spirit through praying in tongues until every thought submits and your Mind aligns with CHRIST.

Aligning the mind to Christ is the reason for Waiting on GOD. It can take hours; it can take days. Therefore, you can start with

216

short times every day and allow it to build up as you maintain the tempo daily until you peak in His Presence. **You can practice Silencing your Mind and all thoughts for 30 mins everyday....**

You can also separate yourself for a personal retreat for a few days, and you can do a marathon for longer days... You can add fasting or not. The primary purpose of fasting is to let your Soul submit to GOD.

In any way you choose to be alone with GOD, let the main focus be to silence your Mind so your Spirit can come alive before GOD. Remember that your Mind cannot worship GOD, and most of the time, when the mind is not renewed, it is anti-GOD.

> *As you spend time alone with GOD, let the focus be on silencing your Mind and shutting out all thoughts.*

As you spend time alone with GOD, let the focus be on silencing your Mind and shutting out all thoughts.

When you start, it may seem difficult and impossible to concentrate at first... however, as you stay at it; eventually, the mind submits to CHRIST. Therefore, the goal of Waiting is to shut out all distractions and thoughts and silence your Mind... so that your Spirit can come alive in CHRIST.

It could take hours; wait until all the wandering thoughts are shut out... This is because most wandering thoughts are sourced from the devil, and as long as you entertain such thoughts during your prayers, CHRIST is not yet real to you.

As you wait, gradually, the thoughts fade off. Your soul becomes silent before GOD; your body and emotion break down. You can begin to cry, weep, agonize or experience a deep feeling of Peace and Rest; that is the breaking point... (It is not the time to stop), It is, however, an indication that you are getting close to the Immersion into the Glory of CHRIST. As you linger on the more, The LIGHT OF THE GOSPEL, WHICH IS THE GLORY OF CHRIST, will shine forth on you. A phenomenon indescribable with words, like the Bible says... 'deep calls unto deep'...

'Deep calls unto deep at the noise of Your waterfalls, All the waves and billows have gone over me.' (Psalms 42:7 NKJV).

You will never remain the same when you taste the Lord's Goodness from His Presence. Now you know how to get there; maybe you stumbled on it before; now you know how you got there... Now, you can replicate this again and again when needed.

Make this a way of life... and the enemy will become a non-issue in your life... Besides, the Best of you will emerge daily beyond your imaginations. Every good thing will begin to submit to you.

Do not be deceived; the enemy will fight this practice with everything they can use: Your close family seeking unnecessary attention, friends setting up strifes, the introduction of distracting pleasure, or a direct attack on your mind to distract you from engaging the Presence of GOD... The reason is apparent, no one accesses the Fullness of CHRIST and remains the same. So, be warned, when you see the oppositions, do not give in, instead,

218

insist on creating the Presence of GOD around you daily. It is the GREATEST WEAPON you can ever have in life –GOD's PRESENCE!

It is an experience you ought to have and enjoy every day. Many stumble on this practice and encounter their miracles; however, because they lack the understanding of how they got it, it becomes difficult to replicate it repeatedly afterwards.

The essence of your Waiting is to get to the point where all thoughts are shut out, and your soul submits to the Lord... This breaking Point can take minutes, hours, days, or weeks ...

When You understand this point, waiting becomes easy, desirous, and effortless as you will pull through to the breaking point!

Start with a sincere love for CHRIST, and spend time in His Presence... Just love His Presence, and let it be regularly... As you do this, less time will be needed to get into 'The Spirit Realm'..., and if you stay on it, very soon, you will Peak into the Glory of CHRIST. My dear friend, what will you rather do with this information?

In our Ministry, we have this exercise we use to practice the Presence of GOD... You can start with this...

The ALMIGHTY FORMULA: 30 MINS HIGH PRAISE ... + 30 MINS WAITING ON THE WORD... + 30 MINS MINGLING WITH THE HOLY SPIRIT... EVERYDAY...

Do this exercise with the consciousness of achieving your goal of waiting on GOD... Silencing the Mind and bringing all thoughts to obey CHRIST.

Set your alarm clock... set it to 30 minutes, then start the exercise. Do not stop each practice until the alarm goes off... It may seem mechanical at first, do not worry; as you get used to redeeming your time from the hand of the evil ones, you will soon no more need the alarm clock, for you will stay put enjoying the Presence of GOD and birthing the FULLNESS of CHRIST for your advantage.

Once it becomes easier to stay focused on Waiting on GOD, you can stop using the alarm or adhering to the 'Almighty Formula'...If you can engage the 'Almighty Formula' for two weeks straight uninterrupted... then it may be time to graduate from the Exercise... Anytime you perceive a distance in your fellowship with GOD, resume the 'Almighty Formula,' and your Spiritual Antenna will come alive. Anytime the enemy throws you a dart that seems overwhelming, Get into the Practice of Waiting on GOD, and you will return with testimonies any day, any time.

When you engage 'The Almighty Formula'... Three main things happen: You usher in GOD's Presence into your life and circumstances; all forces of darkness disappear, and any good thing starts to happen to you. (Miracles, Salvation, Deliverance, Divine breakthroughs and Divine directions -Spiritual Intelligence)

You can start with this exercise, modify it to suit you, or create your own way; all that matters is ... SPEND TIME AND ENGAGE THE FULLNESS OF CHRIST...

For if you do... and long enough, you will discover that absolutely nothing will be impossible with you.

'For it pleased the Father, that in our Lord JESUS CHRIST, all the Fullness should dwell' (Colossians 1:19 NKJV)

No matter what you are faced with, the better part of it is in CHRIST JESUS!

When you make Engaging the Presence of GOD a loving and dwelling place in your life...these scriptures become your reality:

'He who dwells in the secret place of the Most High Shall abide under the shadow of the Almighty.' (Psalms 91:1 NKJV)

'Eye has not seen, Nor ear heard, Nor have entered into the heart of man The things which God has prepared for those who love Him.' (1 Corinthians 2:9)

I pray that this experience becomes your reality in the Name of YESHUA HAMASHIACH (JESUS CHRIST), Amen.

It pleased the Lord that I share this with you, my dear friend...

We Pray that this journey with us has been a BLESSING... Please, endeavour to keep this book copy and go over it again and again until the truth therein becomes your reality.

... doing CHRIST with you has been a BLESSING!

"I am more than the breakthroughs... I am much more than the cars, more than the relationships, more than the family crisis, more than the healings, more than the financial breakthroughs, more than the success, more than the ministry you are running, and whatever you are seeking for or longing after in life...

I am much more than this world...

Eye has not seen, nor ear heard, nor have entered into the heart of man the things which my Father has prepared for those who love Me...

Spend time with Me...

Get to know Me...

I am more than what you will eat, what you will wear, and where you will live...

The best of this present world, at its best, is the least anyone could have...

There is more for My own...

As you seek Me, Dwell with Me, and love My Presence, My Father will love you, and We will come and make Our abode with you...

What you need is My Presence...

What will make a difference is My Presence...

What will stand you out is My Presence...

What the enemy will not be able to stand up against is My Presence...

Long for My Presence...

Seek My Presence...

Make My Presence your Priority...

Make My Presence in your life a daily longing...

The enemy will fight this with everything and with anyone he can...

Nor give place to the enemy...

Resist him, and he will flee from you...

And you will discover that everything others are seeking for will be added unto you...

And you will discover that goodness, riches, abundance, provisions, sound health, deliverance, happiness, peace of mind, pleasure, and long life will be your normal abode...

I will come again...

I will come to take you with Me...

I will come that you may be with Me in My Kingdom forever...

While on this earth, fight the good fight of Faith...

Occupy with My Presence, till I come...   I AM.''

12:41 pm, Wednesday, 11th March 2020

'But seek first the kingdom of God and His righteousness, and all these things shall be added to you.' (Matthew 6:33 NKJV)

'Jesus said to him, 'If you can believe, all things are possible to him who believes.' (Mark 9:23 NKJV)

'For with God nothing will be impossible.' (Luke 1:37 NKJV)

'Hitherto have ye asked nothing in my name; ask, and ye shall receive, that your joy may be full.' (John 16:24 KJV)

'He who has an ear, let him hear what the Spirit says to the Churches.' (Revelation 2:29 NKJV)

Your Notes . . .

The Fullness of CHRIST: What does this mean to you?...

Your Notes . . .

How do you plan to engage the Fullness of CHRIST in your life?

Notes

PRAYER OF SALVATION ...

Lord Jesus, I believe you are the SON of GOD that came to the world. You died on the cross for all Sins, Iniquities, and Transgressions. Your BLOOD redeemed man from all sins, and their consequences, from all curses, delivered man from the authority of darkness and translated them into your kingdom.

[8]I believe I, therefore, receive and confess you JESUS CHRIST as my Lord and Saviour. Thank you for dying for me and forgiven me of my sins. I receive by faith the forgiveness of my sins. I receive authority, the power to become a son of GOD, with the Gift of Righteousness, a Right Standing with GOD. I am delivered from Satan and all the forces of darkness. I am a new creature now; old things are passed away. Everything becomes new, thank you, Lord; I am born again. Amen. Alleluia.

Lord JESUS, you said you would send the HOLY SPIRIT to help, teach, comfort, strengthen, and reveal all truth to us. Now that I am born again, I ask by faith for the HOLY GHOST's Baptism in JESUS's Name, Amen. Thank you because I have received HIM. Now, HE is mine; I give you GLORY, Amen. I speak by faith and trust that the HOLY SPIRIT gives me UTTERANCE now in JESUS NAME, AMEN.

---

[8] For further support on your salvation, contact us: Email: info@air.church

THANK YOU . . .

_____

Thank you for reading this piece. We pray that it BLESSES you as it is BLESSING us too...

My dear friend, what will you rather do with this information?

Please share your experiences with us, email us at info@air.church and let us hear how this book has helped improve your prayer life. Thank you for the opportunity to share with you.

Expecting your testimonies. . .

Our GOD is GOOD, and HIS MERCIES endure forevermore, Amen.

I have MERCY; I obtain MERCY, Amen

... pst tomowo

... setting men up with GOD, for a Glorious Turnaround.

some more ...

JESUS CHRIST... my Substitute, my Sacrifice, my Inheritance...

it starts with a substitution, followed by the sacrifice, then the inheritance. Until Christians lay hold on this truth, questions and doubts around the realities of CHRIST's existence and purpose for mankind will linger on . . ..

I'm a STAR! . . .
Managing the gifting and the gifted

Gifting can be as little as your name always come up...Many gifted people are bullied, oppressed, suppressed, simply because people around them lack the understanding of WHY and HOW to manage the gift

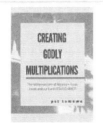

Creating GODLY Multiplications

The hidden secrets of Abraham, Isaac, Jacob and our Lord JESUS CHRIST to GODLY Multiplications. Also revealing how one can apply them in today's world and circumstances.

The LIFE Coaching ...

This is an online coaching platform with pst tomowo, an online retreat where we set men up with GOD for a Glorious Turnaround.

*For more information on these ... Email us: **info@air.church**

Notes . . .

MEET PST TOMOWO ···

'Tomowo Faduyile George (pst tomowo) is a passionate lover of GOD.

A dynamic and prophetic teacher of the WORD with vivid presence of GOD's Anointing. A trained pharmacist, expert in public health, a lover of people, team player, peace-loving, gentle and beautiful lady.

pst tomowo is called into teaching and ministering of GOD's GRACE, endowed with GOD's Presence, Power and Goodness.

She is known for her soft touch of motherly love, ready to Give, BLESS and Support.

Having been through and overcome several long standing, personal challenges, HELPED by GOD, pst tomowo pulls from this depth, always armed with a sweet smile and a word of encouragement for anyone that meets her, every time.

She is easily drawn to people in need, especially women, young adults and children.

She is a Life Coach, an author, artist, dynamic teacher of the Word, runs an all-online Faith based LIFE Coaching, accessible worldwide for retreats, self helps, mentoring and encounters for breakthrough... She also runs other online broadcasts.